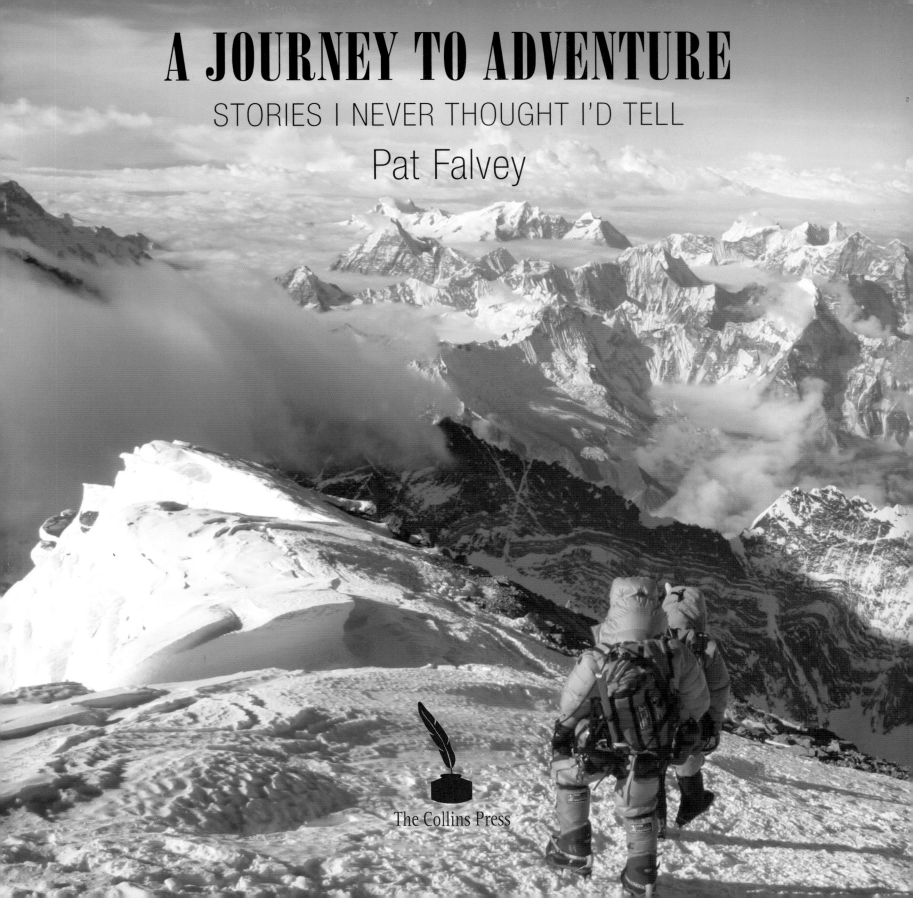

A JOURNEY TO ADVENTURE
STORIES I NEVER THOUGHT I'D TELL

Pat Falvey

The Collins Press

Published in 2007 by
The Collins Press
West Link Park
Doughcloyne
Wilton
Cork
Ireland

British Library Cataloguing in Publication Data

Falvey, Pat, 1957-
A journey to adventure : stories I never thought I'd tell
1. Falvey, Pat, 1957- 2. Mountaineering 3. Mountaineers –

     Ireland – Biography

     I. Title

     796.5'22'092

     ISBN-13: 9781905172535

Book, jacket design and typesetting by Burns Design except back cover by Bright Idea.

Font: Sabon 10.5/16

Printed in Ireland

Title page: Clare O'Leary with Sherpa descending from Everest Summit.

Facing page: A climbing Sherpa on Ama Dablam.

Butter candles in a Buddhist temple in Kathmandu. People seeking peace and tranquillity light these candles.

To Marie, Brian and Patrick

'There's a breed of men that don't fit in, A breed that can't keep still,
So they break the heart of kith and kin and roam the world at will.
They range the field and rove the flood and climb the mountains' crest,
for theirs' is the blood of the gypsy's curse for they don't know when to rest.'

ROBERT SERVICE

CONTENTS

Practising ice climbing in the Val d'Aosta in the Italian Alps.

HOW MANY OF US DREAM, but never get around to making our dreams a reality. Too many people go through life afraid to live the lives they'd like to live, only to find one day that it's too late to do something about it — life has passed them by. But when, exactly, is too late

I know this sounds like a cliché, but I really believe that life is not a rehearsal, but a performance – **we're only going to get one shot, so we'd better make the most of it.** That is how I have endeavoured to live my life. I am now 50 years of age – and I've spent the last half-century taking risks, seeking adventure, and living on the edge in both my business and personal life. These years have been a rollercoaster ride of highs and lows: moments of extraordinary success and achievement, and dips into failure and loss.

So far, my adventures have taken me to nearly every corner of the planet. As I look through a vast collection of photographs, the memories and stories come rushing back.

Sometimes what I recall about my adventures are the mountains themselves, and the challenges I faced climbing them. Other times, it's the colourful scenery or wildlife that I recall. I have had the opportunity to meet so many interesting people, and learn about their ways of life. I've learned that the human drive to seek adventure is universal. This bond we share is what makes me remember the friends I have made — and sometimes lost — on expeditions.

I'm often asked how it feels to stand on the peaks of the Seven Summits, or the top of Mount Everest. Of course, it's absolutely brilliant. To think for a small time in the history of our earth that you are the highest person on each of the seven continents is almost beyond words. But these expeditions are not without their tragedies. I have lost friends that had similar dreams and aspirations to mine, because they too followed a call to adventure.

I am often bombarded with negatives: 'It can't be done', 'it's impossible', 'you'll die', 'you're getting too old – you'd think that at your age you should have more sense ...' Although I listen to advice, I always follow my own beliefs in the end.

Looking back, I believe I was imbued with drive and determination as a very young child. I went to live with my grandmother at six years of age and she set me up with my first business, buying me a pram to collect second-hand clothes for her to sell as a carter. Later I would deliver turf to old-age pensioners for three pence a bag. My grandmother drummed into me the art of hard work. Her abiding lesson then was, *If you think you can you will, if you think you can't you won't, so always believe in what you're doing.*

And so I have.

Follow your dreams and make them a reality.

August 2007

Seven ladders tied together in the Khumbu Ice Fall to ascend one of the many ice walls approaching Camp 1 from Everest Base Camp.

Facing page – clockwise from top left: Pat Falvey, aged four, with his grandmother Mary B; Pat Falvey (left) and friend, Joe O'Leary, relaxing in the mid 1990s; Buddhist monks en route to Everest Base Camp for the puja ceremony to appease the gods of the mountain; Pat Falvey training at Vinterogvar in Norway in spring 2007.

CARRAUNTOOHIL & TRAINING

Carrauntoohil / Corrán Tuathail
County Kerry, Ireland
MacGillycuddy's Reeks Range
1,039 metres

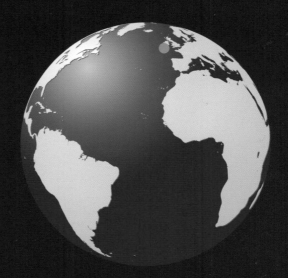

HAVING TRAVELLED THE WORLD and been to some amazing places, I have found no place like home. The beauty of the landscape in Ireland, its lush green hillsides and valleys, its dark lakes and endless rivers and streams provide havens of tranquillity.

My appreciation for home has grown year after year as I see more clearly the positive attributes of Ireland. Travel has broadened my mind. There was a time when I felt Ireland was not an interesting place to live — but now, having experienced what other places in the world have to offer, I appreciate the things that are good about Ireland.

I love planning expeditions and travelling, but more than anything I love coming home. Even when on expedition, my mind always runs through places back home I never tire of seeing, walking or climbing: the offshore islands, the Blaskets, the Skellig Islands, the glaciated valleys of the Reeks and the Gap of Dunloe.

LEARNING TO WALK ALL OVER AGAIN

I didn't always have such an appreciation for my surroundings. I used to rush everywhere, constantly using clichés like 'I don't have a minute'. Now I realise there are 10,080 minutes in a week, and I probably had a few to spare – even back then.

Twenty years ago, when I was battling to save a failing business and keep my family home, I was introduced to the hills of Kerry through the intervention of Val Deane. I didn't know how to get out of the dilemma I had created for myself, and I was at my lowest ebb. Val was the father of my secretary, Valerie, and he dropped in one morning to 'cheer me up'. His message, however, was not one I was the least bit interested in hearing.

I was a true workaholic back then. I couldn't fathom why someone would spend time tramping over hillsides for no financial or material reward. But Val was an avid hillwalker, and he had an idea that this was exactly the medicine I needed. He did not simply invite me to the mountains, or suggest I get some fresh air. Val literally pestered me onto the hills of Kerry.

Facing page: Two climbers on Howling Ridge, Carrauntoohil, in winter conditions.
Above: Walking in the Black Valley (left) and the Gap of Dunloe (right).

Pat Falvey walking near Carrauntoohil in snowy conditions.

Five days and a gentle reminder from Val later, I was travelling west to Kerry with Val and a gang of climbers from Cork Mountaineering Club – one of Cork's first hillwalking clubs. Our objective was a small mountain in County Kerry called Mangerton. My fellow passengers were downright giddy and gleeful, looking forward to their day out. Deep in my own thoughts I wondered at their excitement.

Standing atop Mangerton that day, however, I found that I felt more alive than I had in years. Upon reaching the summit, the mood was merry and cheerful – the other walkers smiled and offered their heart-felt congratulations, warmly shaking my hand. I had to admit, I was elated. For the first time in months I had set my sights on a goal and achieved my objective, and I felt proud. I was tired, but I had succeeded in climbing my first mountain. I had no idea how much this moment would reshape my future.

It wasn't just the sense of achievement that excited me. Taking time to relax on the mountain top, I became tuned in to nature for the first time in my life. I focused on the beauty that surrounded me. I listened to the water flowing over the rocks. I watched tufts of grass ruffle in the breeze. I took in the muted colours of the bog, in sharp contrast to the blue of the sky. I followed the line of a stream running down the hill and caught sight of the Lakes of Killarney.

COMING ALIVE IN KERRY

I was hooked by the time we gathered up to head back down the mountain. Ready to go wherever they were headed the following week, I was surprised and excited to hear next Sunday's destination was Carrauntoohil, the highest mountain in Ireland. Descending Mangerton, I listened intently as the other climbers discussed next week's climb. They spoke of steep scree-covered slopes, knife-edged ridges, gusting winds, and even deaths on the mountains.

After ringing Val several times the next week to see if our journey to the top of Carrauntoohil was still on (chuckling at our role reversal), we travelled once again to Kerry. Carrauntoohil was everything I had hoped. Val was my climbing partner that day, and stayed with me every step of the way, making sure I was safe.

On the summit I turned to my companion and proclaimed, 'Val, I am going to climb Everest one of these days'. He just smiled and said nothing.

Years later, Val admitted to thinking at that moment that I was totally out of touch with reality. He couldn't believe anybody would have the cheek to climb two small mountains and then say they would climb Everest. But for me, even then, it was no delusion. I wanted to pick something that seemed unachievable. Then and there I had made my mind up, as my grandmother's wise words came into my head – 'If you think you can, you will. If you think you can't, you won't.'

From that point on, a love affair with the mountains began that has never faded. It was lucky for me Val interfered in my life. I'm not sure that anybody at the time knew just how low my self-confidence was.

Now, I have often gazed down from the peak of Carrauntoohil. My home sits perched on a hill at the western boundary of Killarney National Park, with my back garden as Ireland's highest mountain range. Although every approach to this mountain is just as magical, my favourite is to ascend up Howling Ridge, an arête which gives some of the best climbing in Ireland. I also really enjoy getting a small group together for a night walk to the summit. We set out before sunrise, crest each peak in the Reeks, and time our walk to arrive at the iron cross of Carrauntoohil just as the sun rises.

There was a time my ambition was conquering the highest mountains, seeking out the most remote regions and reaching the poles. Although I still do plenty of exploring, my interests have changed to taking people into the hills, mountains, glaciers and deserts of this world, so that they can experience what I have felt and where I have found peace.

Above left: Pat Falvey on an early trip to the hills.

To Val, my mentor, I pay tribute to his foresight for introducing me to the challenge of mountaineering. Val sadly died on 26 September 2006 at the early age of 72. Thank you Val. May you rest in peace.

Val Deane holds an ice axe that Pat Falvey used on Everest.

WELCOME TO KERRY

To this day, each time I pass the 'Welcome to Kerry' sign again at the county boundary, my spirits rise. During those early years of living in Cork, crossing the 'county bounds' into Kerry meant I could relax. When I crossed that line, I could forget my troubles. The result was that a day of walking and climbing in a totally uncluttered and natural environment cleared my mind, leaving me better able to solve problems.

Skellig Michael

Previous pages:

Left page – Climbing on Howling Ridge.

Right page –

Top: Carrauntoohil from Beenkeragh showing l. to r. Curved, Central and O'Shea's gullies. (Photo courtesy Jim Ryan, author of *Carrauntoohil & MacGillycuddy's Reeks*).

Bottom left: Winter climbing on Howling Ridge.

Bottom right: A winter climb in Curved Gully on Carrauntoohil.

President Mary McAleese on the summit of Carrauntoohil with husband Martin and daughter Emma. On the right are Mick O'Connell, the famous Kerry footballer and his son Micheál.

Sunset from Carrauntoohil in winter.

Sunrise walking near Ireland's highest mountain on the Reeks.

Pat rescuing a German shepherd stranded on a cliff in Cork City.

WAY BACK WHEN...

AT THE BEGINNING OF MY CLIMBING CAREER, the fundamental skills I needed to learn to survive on the mountains were many. Because of the variety of expeditions I wanted to be involved with, I knew I would have to learn all the disciplines required.

It was a long and daunting list: rock and ice climbing, fixed rope techniques, crevasse rescue, sled pulling, camp craft, navigation, jummaring and so on. I would also need to learn ladder techniques, traditional and satellite navigation by GPS (Global Positioning System), snow shoeing, skiing, kiting on skis and mountain first aid, avalanche risk assessment and evacuation. Mental training and preparation would be required, as well as logistical planning, and finally, the dread of dealing with casualties and death on the mountain.

Not all of these could be learned in Ireland. I knew that I would need to travel to other countries. But how could I possibly get this experience, and where would I meet and learn from people who also had a love for my new sport

I began by joining courses on navigation and mountain leadership. I also learned to judge weather. Fortunately, these courses involved an outing with the Kerry Mountain Rescue team. I met Con Moriarty, and through Con I was invited to join Kerry Mountain Rescue. For anyone wishing to learn mountain craft, joining a volunteer rescue group is an excellent way to accelerate the process. My team members became friends that I still climb with twenty years later.

A Search and Rescue helicopter assisting Kerry Mountain Rescue by simulating an airlift.

Top: Kerry Mountain Rescue team in action.
Middle: Training expedition members in Kerry.
Bottom: Developing mountaineering winter skills with a group in Scotland.

For training we travelled to Scotland and the French Alps as well as climbing locally to learn rock-climbing skills. For nine years I was involved with Kerry Mountain Rescue. We trained an average of six weekends every year, and worked together in our time off to practise. Dealing with numerous injuries and fatalities on the Kerry hills also taught us to respect safety on the mountains.

We play in a dangerous sport and I would hate to think that I – or any of my team members on an expedition – would lack the skills to save someone's life. I have been lucky in this regard: the first time I attempted Everest from the south side, I ran into trouble near the top. I was suffering from high-altitude cerebral oedema, and had lost my peripheral vision. Thankfully, when my team members discovered me in a very bad state, they were skilled enough to help me down the mountain. If they hadn't, I would not be here to tell this story.

'All men dream, but not equally. Those who dream by night in the dusty recesses of their minds wake in the day to find that it was vanity: but the dreamers of the day are dangerous men, for they may act their dreams with open eyes, to make it possible. This I did'.

LAWRENCE OF ARABIA

Practising ice climbing in the French Alps.

Left: Sunrise in the Swiss Alps.

AMA DABLAM

Eastern Nepal

Himalaya Range

6,856 metres

AMA DABLAM

I CAN SEE IT, FEEL IT, as clearly as if it were yesterday. The new millennium was only a few weeks away, and I was just 50 metres from the summit of Ama Dablam. A towering, lofty place, I was nearing the top of a spectacular mountain peak on my second attempt. I had worked hard to get there: this day began many hours earlier from our tiny High Camp some 400 metres (1,300 feet) below, at the base of a 60- to 70-degree wall of ice. The past couple of days had been challenging, with very technical and demanding climbing.

This mountain is a special place for my climbing partner Con Moriarty and I, where so much began and finished for us. Events took place here that marked great changes in our lives. I always thought of Ama Dablam as Con's mountain, and had come back this second time to climb it with him.

The first time I was invited to climb this mountain was in 1991. Con had received permission from the Nepalese government to attempt Ama Dablam. He asked if I would be interested, and I accepted in a flash. My head was spinning. I had read books, seen films and dreamed about going to the Himalaya. I couldn't believe that now I was actually going.

Con put together a team for the expedition. Six climbers, Con Moriarty, Pat Falvey, Tony Farrell, Mike Shea, Ciarán Corrigan and Mick Murphy, one Base Camp manager, Tim Hickey, and three support trekkers made up our expedition.

Ama Dablam seen from Pangboche in the Khumbu Valley.

AMA DABLAM

Ama Dablam: Mother and her Necklace, Mother's Charm Box, Mother's Jewel Box. 'Ama' means mother, grandmother or even world. 'Dablam' means charm box, and is a special pendant worn by elder Sherpa women that holds precious items. The mountain has a hanging glacier that resembles a dablam and the two extending ridges are outstreched like a maternal embrace.

The earliest reconnaissance into the Himalaya focused on finding a way up Everest, but en route many of these early pioneers were awestruck by dozens of other peaks in the area. All were lower in elevation than the mighty Chomolungma, but were giants compared to any western peaks. Most went unnamed and un-surveyed and, of course, none were climbed.

A number of these jagged points, where the summit icicles seemed to pierce the sky, looked far more beautiful than Mount Everest herself. In future years, the race to summit the very highest mountains in the world by the leading mountaineering nations slowed down a little. When it did, these smaller and highly technical peaks – deemed outrageous only a few years earlier – would attract a new generation of climbers ready to make bold ascents of the steep walls, ridges and faces.

There was one peak in Nepal, however, that stood out for all who saw it. Dove-like in appearance, it has four great faces and four ribbon-like ridges aligned with the principal points on a compass. Standing alone as a steep sentinel to the goddess herself, the local population believed it to be the dwelling of powerful spirits. The mighty hanging glacier below the summit on the west face reminded them of the Ama Dablam, or mother's charm box worn by their women folk, and so they named it. The mountain's stunning shape seemed like a magnificent sculpture and looked indeed a sacred creation.

Eric Shipton, Everest expedition leader, declared Ama Dablam un-climbable while training for the first Everest ascent in the 1950s. Since then it has fuelled the imaginations of climbers. The first successful ascent was in 1961 by Michael Gill and Wally Romanes, Sr. from New Zealand, Barry Bishop from the US and Michael Ward of the UK. Steep and technical, it is known to climbers as the Matterhorn of the Himalayas for its soaring ridges and steep faces. Its summit stands at 6,856 metres (22,830 feet).

The team, front (from left): Mike Shea, Ciarán Corrigan, Mick Murphy and Con Moriarty; back (from left): Tim Hickey, Pat Falvey and Tony Farrell.

Female Sherpa porters (Sherpani) on the Everest trail.

INTO KATHMANDU

The starting point for expeditions to many of the great Himalayan Peaks is Kathmandu. Arriving in this bustling city the first time caused a sensory overload. People were hustling, pulling us aside, beckoning us here, there – for someone who had never been outside Europe, the smells, sounds and sights were like nothing I could have imagined. We walked through the busy streets and markets of Thamel, in the old region of the city. While there, we visited some of the famous and awe-inspiring temples of the Hindus.

SUCCESSES AND DANGERS

That first year our expedition was able to boast the only successful summit of Ama Dablam for the season, but we also experienced failure. Con and Mike suffered terribly from a case of botulism from a can of tainted pineapples purchased in Kathmandu. Camp 2 was as far as they got. Tony Farrell and I had broken through the crux of the mountain, and had reached a ledge just below the Mushroom Ridge at around 20,000 feet (6,096 metres). We let Mick Murphy and Ciaran Corrigan take over to push up the mountain to Camp 3 to attempt the summit. After a bold ascent, Mick Murphy reached the summit alone, while his partner Corrigan descended – suffering terribly from acute mountain sickness. Mick got frostbite on his toes during his descent.

HIGH ALTITUDE EVACUATION

It was amazing that Ciaran was able to descend, let alone live while we waited for help. We sent a distress call for a helicopter, and waited a full week for it to arrive. An evacuation at this height meant the chopper had to push beyond its limits. They emptied everything they possibly could out of the helicopter and used only the minimum of fuel. A full-scale emergency evacuation ensued, with both men airlifted to Kathmandu.

Throughout the wait for an evacuation, a seemingly endless barrage of storms hit the mountain, which beat back any further attempts at climbing. The team eventually decided to call it a day, happy at the fact that we succeeded as a team to reach the summit.

Ciarán Corrigan (right), suffering from pulmonary oedema, returning to Base Camp.

Kathmandu was once again the starting place for our 1999 expedition. This time, instead of trekking the full way in, our little team of Con Moriarty, his brother Denis, a friend Ann Curran and I flew into the tiny airstrip at Lukla in the Khumbu. As the small plane weaved in and around the hills, we enjoyed stunning views of some of the greatest mountains in the world. Continuing up the valley, Everest came into sight, with its great plume of jet stream blowing from the summit northwards into Tibet. On foot, our path took us on a relentless uphill through rhododendron forests and away from habitation.

DISASTER ON MERA

To get used to the altitude, we decided to first climb Mera Peak (6,476 metres, 21,246 feet) a popular, technically easy alpine-style climb. If our plan worked, we would arrive at Ama Dablam fully acclimatised, ready to make a rapid ascent.

Climbing through the pass to our camp gave us the first feel of snow on this trip. It felt great to be in our crampons, but Con was struggling with the altitude. Later that night the weather changed dramatically and the pressure fell. It began to snow heavily, burying our tents. The pain in Con's head continued to worsen throughout the night.

When day broke, we discovered the reality of the storm that had passed. Three metres of snow had fallen overnight. The whole landscape was unrecognisable from the evening before. With Con's suffering we would need to descend as soon as possible. Our only option was to get out of there, in the direction from which we

The train of Sherpas, trekkers and climbers in the storm on the Mera La. Not everyone made it back safely due to snow blindness, frostbite and death.

had come. A few Sherpas and I began cutting a trail. We were aware that many of the porters and Sherpas on the other teams did not have the equipment or gear to survive for any length of time in these conditions. Most of the other groups who were in the area to climb Mera realised they, too would have to abandon their trek, and a long line of 85 people followed in our trail. Ten or so were Western trekkers, and the rest were Sherpas and others working on various trips. White-out conditions caused zero visibility, and the powder-soft snow meant we progressed exceptionally slowly. Con was at the very rear, struggling to keep everyone moving.

It was bitterly cold and soon we noticed people tiring, especially porters who were hopelessly under-dressed in cottons and running shoes. They were in dire circumstances, so we began to break open our packs to treat those worst affected.

We made very slow progress. Someone called out that a man had died — it was a Sherpa from one of the groups following. His name was Lhakpa Sherpa from the village of Kharikhola. He was a high-altitude Sherpa who grew up at 2,600 metres and worked his whole life on the heights. During the previous night he suffered a bad headache and by daybreak, cerebral oedema had set in.

In disbelief, we continued in the surreal atmosphere of the storm, as wind and snow whipped around us. Then somebody said that a kitchen boy had died too. I asked one of our Sherpas where the bodies were, and was told that they would be left in tents until the snows passed, when their families could come and retrieve them.

This was one of the first times I questioned the logic of why we put ourselves in situations like this. Above us were thousands of tons of fresh snow, precariously perched on steep slopes. And if the weather got any worse, or if the wind picked up …

Some five hours after leaving camp, we had only reached the other side of the Mera La. Con had taken the lead at this point, and for the rest of the afternoon we worked harder than we ever had in our lives to find a way through boulder fields and down steep slopes. Nearly twelve hours after setting out, we arrived at the old summer pasture huts of Khare where we'd stayed two nights ago. The Sherpas were familiar enough with the terrain to know where the Yak herders' huts were, and dug with their bare hands until they found the roofs, and eventually the simple shelters underneath.

The next day we did what we could, then turned to get out of the Hinku Valley as fast as we could. Soon we learned that the death toll of that storm was around a dozen, all Sherpa men who died working on trekking and climbing holidays. Altitude sickness, avalanches and cold killed them on a variety of mountains.

Far too many mountaineers and trekkers have a pathetic disregard for the welfare of their staff and each year men die in these mountains, carrying loads of 'comfort toys' that cost more than the Sherpas will earn in a year. None of us would be anywhere near these peaks without the support of Sherpas who, in recent years, have built businesses providing the necessary services. However, in a land where life is cheap, many are severely abused and lack basic protection.

We headed back to Lukla and had never been happier to have a hot shower and a few pints. We set out for Ama Dablam as soon as we had rested, travelling along the footpath to Everest.

THE SHERPA PEOPLE

Living in the Solo Khumbu area, the Sherpa (meaning man from the east) are one of the many ethnic groups in Nepal and India. They have their own language, traditions, cultural heritage and religion. They live amongst the deep, fertile valleys that have been cut by massive rivers flowing through some of the highest mountains in the world.

The Sherpa people are considered some of the strongest climbers and porters. Although most clearly associated with Everest, they have earned a name for their community and country as a whole by conquering some of the other gigantic peaks that surround their homes. They are a happy, free people that practice their religious beliefs as part of their living day. Of all the world's cultures I've travelled with, the Sherpa are among the most religious, hospitable and friendly.

Camps 1, 2 and 3 on Ama Dablam.

The main route to Everest had changed so much since we walked here in 1991. We found it busier, and were pleased to see that greater wealth was apparent among the Sherpa. Women operating stalls where we bought apple tarts a few years back welcomed us as friends and showed us around their new, improved homes. Their young children attended the local Hillary primary schools, and teenagers were educated in the high schools of Kathmandu. They now had telephones, and we were even able to send email from the Sherpa trading town of Namche Bazarr.

Five days out of Lukla we strolled into the familiar Mingbo Valley. A steep ascent alongside a riverbed placed us at the foot of the most beautiful mountain I know. As I walked, my eyes were fixed firmly on the right-hand skyline of Ama Dablam. I recognised its features so well and yearned to feel them again.

After resting at Base Camp for a day, we began ferrying loads of gear, food and fuel to Camp 1 at the foot of the Southwest Ridge. The views from this camp were superb. There, tucked below the knife-edge on a series of stone-built platforms, we lashed our tents down. All around us were white peaks of rock and ice, glistening in the last rays of the sunset. When the sun shone up here, the temperatures were pleasant – in the mid-twenties – but minutes after sundown it plummeted to minus twenty degrees Celsius and below.

The ridge itself looked amazing, steep and intimidating, but friendly as we became reacquainted with places etched on our brains. The summit looked near and we felt great. We rested and prepared. Later that night Con developed a terrible headache and further symptoms of altitude sickness. He gasped for air amidst attacks of empty retching all night. At daybreak he packed and began his descent back to Base Camp. He would go down to recover and be back tomorrow.

The plan was that I would hang out at Camp 1, wait for Con to return and we would make our bid then. I could see from his attitude as he gave me a hug before he left that he was trying to fight off the mental negativity that comes when sick. 'I'll be back tomorrow Falvey, I just need to rest a day at Base Camp.' The problem was that our time was running out, and both of us feared another storm would break before we could attempt the summit. I watched him from my vantage point as he disappeared into the distance, stumbling down along the ridge, resting regularly on his poles.

Despite descending 5,000 feet, Con's condition deteriorated. At Base Camp, he actually got worse. The following day he attempted an ascent to get back up to me, only to face a near total refusal by his body to push beyond an hour out.

That night he spoke to me on the radio and pleaded with me to make my summit bid the first chance I got. He had no idea when he would be able to get up to where I was, and knew I wouldn't be doing myself any favours staying too long at 20,000 feet.

Facing page: Camp 1 on the West Ridge at 18,900 feet.

Left: The traverse from Camp 1 to 2 at the Yellow Tower, just below Camp 2 at 19,500 feet.

Top: Pat Falvey on the knife-edge Mushroom Ridge from Camps 2 to 3.

Bottom: Carrying heavy loads on the traverse at 19,000 feet.

Facing page: Climbing the difficult ice barrel leading to the final summit slope.

Above: Resting at the crux on the steep ice face of the Dablam below the summit.

I decided to go for it the following day. I was strong and comfortable with the task ahead. I wanted to go for a fast ascent and decided that I'd push directly from Camp 1 to 3, which is situated below the hanging glacier. I would then go for the summit in the early hours the following morning. My decision was made easier when I heard that two Scottish climbers and their Sherpas, Dave Cummings, Kate Ross, Phendon and Pemba, were also going out onto the ridge the following day. I would join them on my ascent. I tried to focus on keeping a steady foothold as we crossed an incredibly narrow ridge with drop-offs of thousands of feet on either side. Weaving in and around smaller pinnacles of granite and absailing over the bigger ones was spectacular.

The position of Camp 2 on the Yellow Tower provided heart-stopping views. This is where I had to turn back in 1991 and, entering the sheer ice gully beyond, I felt excited to explore the unknown territory that had lived only in my imagination for ten years. The gully led around the Mushroom Ridge, and with its double cornice led us right under the Dablam hanging glacier.

Climbing around the Dablam was very steep. The ice was old and black and my toes hurt from kicking so hard. It was here that my big toes got a little frost bitten, but in the intense concentration I didn't notice. Making progress toward the summit I was frozen to my core but comfortable in my airy position, and I finally reached Camp 3, set up my tent, and fell asleep for the night.

Crawling out of my tent the next day, I was amazed by the majestic views. We would push for the summit from here. At the top of the Dablam, I crossed the bergshrund formed by thousands of tons of ice that hang in a great lump. It looked to me like a blob some giant had thrown at the mountain. Mick Murphy must have spent a long, cold night in this dark crack on his descent in 1999.

It had taken nineteen days to get to this point since we began our walk in. My mind raced with thoughts of Con far below, of returning home, and suddenly, I discovered I couldn't climb any higher! I was standing on the top.

Cresting one wall of this peak, another almost immediately drops away. It is so pointy and narrow up here – an abode of the gods all right. For over ten years I had dreamed of standing on this peak! It was as if I was standing on an island and all around me was a sea – a sea of mountains everywhere, north, south, east and west.

As I sat there pondering this tremendous achievement, I received a tap on the shoulder. It was a paraglider! With a wink, he launched, and in seconds he was in mid-air, hanging from his threads some 8,000 feet over our Base Camp! His flight was like that of an eagle. It seemed so effortless and I envied that he would be drinking tea at Base Camp in only minutes. Con told me later that, after a 25-minute flight, he glided onto the snow near camp and – in a landing akin to a James Bond scene – planted a kiss on the lips of his girlfriend as he touched down!

Con came out to greet me when I returned to Base Camp. Tears came to my eyes and I'm sure Con knew why. I had felt guilty at summiting without him. As we hugged, Con cried too, and I knew that he was struggling to make sense of how he had failed to acclimatise on this trip and had once again been robbed of the summit. He turned to me and said, his voice breaking, 'It's OK Falvey … it was not meant to be this time'.

The paraglider departing the summit of Ama Dablam.

Clare O'Leary on the summit.

From the first time I set eyes on Ama Dablam, I decided I would climb it. It is one of the most aesthetic mountains I have ever seen. In May 2006, I took a trip to the Himalayas, and after acclimatising on Pokalde, I headed for Ama Dablam. Pat's original plans to have an Irish team on the mountain didn't work out, so I decided to climb it with two Sherpa friends only. I had heard many stories about this amazing mountain from Pat and Con Moriarty, and I was very excited, but apprehensive.

The climb was amazing, the route spectacular and the conditions tough. It was strange not having the support of a team, but things went well and on 17 May we reached the summit. Ours were the final summits of the season – a snow storm the following day closed the mountain for the spring season. I was delighted things worked in my favour on that trip – it was nice to be on the mountain, making decisions and taking responsibility for them.

CLARE O'LEARY

EVEREST NORTH SIDE

Tibet
Mahalangur Himal
Himalaya
8,848 metres

EVEREST NORTH SIDE

THE DESIRE TO STAND at the highest point on earth has fired the imagination and fuelled the enthusiasm of climbers throughout the world, and will do so for generations to come. When I think about my experiences, nothing can come close to the two times in my life when I stood on the highest point on earth.

Since I first set foot on Mount Everest in 1993, this mountain has moulded my life as an adventurer. I have been there four times, and have seen its raw natural beauty – both its serenity and ferocity. Friends have died on Everest because they had a similar passion for this mountain. On my first visit I buried one of my team mates on the East Rongbuk Glacier. Years later, I nearly died in the rarefied atmosphere high on the mountain. Reaching 28,750 feet, at the base of the infamous Hillary step in 2003, I had to make the hardest decision of my life: to return just one hour from the summit. But the joys far outweighed the pains for me when I first stood on that sacrosanct piece of ground in 1995 and again in 2004. I was in awe of my airy position and the unfolding sights as I turned 360 degrees – north, south, east and west. I was completely aware of my position as my emotions ran wild. To those who live beneath Everest she is called *Chomolungma*, which translates as 'Goddess Mother of our Earth'. Reaching the summit is a spiritual experience for locals, and I felt that same connection.

MOUNT EVEREST / Chomolungma is the highest mountain on Earth, as measured by the height of its summit above sea level. The mountain, which is part of the Himalaya range in High Asia, is located on the border between Nepal and Tibet, China. As of the end of the 2006 climbing season, there have been 3,050 ascents to the summit, by 2,062 individuals, and 203 people have died on the mountain.

Mount Everest from the Rongbuk Glacier Base Camp.

Base Camp after a fresh snowfall on the Rongbuk Glacier.

Sherpa children training to be porters!

Pat Falvey with fellow climbers in a truck en route to Base Camp.

TO REACH THE SUMMIT

I have climbed this mountain from both Tibet and Nepal, following the original routes of the first successful summits by man.

Mallory and Irvine pioneered the North/Northeast face of Everest, from the Tibet side. Of course, the question that has always intrigued people is: were they the first to climb Everest, or not.

From the south in Nepal, I have followed the route that Hillary and Tenzing took in 1953, when they achieved the historical distinction of becoming the first to reach the top of the world.

DANGER ON EVEREST

Now that I have reached the summit from both Nepal and Tibet, I can honestly say *there is no easy way to climb Mount Everest*. We know more about the mountain now, and the gear we use is better, but the dangers are the same as they have always been. One could say even *more* dangerous. In addition to all the natural instability of weather, avalanches, rock fall, landslides and crevasses, there are now other, more frightening dangers to contend with: inexperienced climbers that go to the mountain ill prepared.

In 2004, on our summit day, three people died on the mountain, and controversy arose about one guide.

He had been promised a $20,000 bonus if he successfully reached the summit with his client. The team did reach the summit, but on their descent the client was so exhausted that the guide had to make a decision to leave him on The Balcony. The two Sherpas with them later described how the client had begged not to be left behind. On their return to High Camp a rescue was mounted to go back up to The Balcony, but the weather conditions had changed for the worst. The rescue had to be aborted. Two days later, an English team searched for the person on The Balcony but never found him.

So Everest now attracts all types of people with different agendas, and will do so in the future unless regulated to a code of practice.

AN AMAZING FEELING

As long as Everest is the highest mountain in the world, it will attract the experienced, inexperienced, those on spiritual quests and those that make their living from it. But there is one thing for sure, and that is, whether you're the first like Hillary and Tenzing, or the thousandth person to stand on the peak, you will be, for that short period in the history of our planet, the highest person on Earth. You will have played a game of Russian roulette in an arena that has no mercy on the weak, or those who are in the wrong place at the wrong time.

NORTH SIDE, 1993

My dream of Everest started on small mountains in Kerry, and within seven years I was on my way. I had trained hard, had become a proficient mountaineer, and was really confident of my ability to achieve my goal. I was invited on an expedition by Mark Miller, from England, who I had befriended while climbing in Scotland. Sadly, Mark died in a plane crash while on reconnaissance in Nepal for the expedition. Jon Tinker, a seasoned and accomplished mountaineer, took over the position. For me, this expedition into high altitude was to be a steep learning curve, and the lessons I learned would not be forgotten.

That year I did not summit Everest. However, our team was very successful. John Tinker, Majic Berbaka, Ang-Babu Chiri and Lharpa Sherpa reached the summit. I had worked very hard on the mountain and reached 8,200 metres without supplementary oxygen. I was at a height equivalent to the sixth highest mountain in the world when I was forced to turn due to the high jet stream winds. I felt good at this altitude, and I knew I could manage the other 600 metres if I returned.

DEATH OF A TEAM MATE

That year I had a traumatic experience. One of our team, Karl Henize, an American astronaut and scientist, was undertaking a scientific project on the mountain. Karl developed high-altitude mountain sickness after just arriving at Advanced Base Camp, at the top of the East Rongbuk Glacier at 21,000 feet. We did our best to rescue

Climbing on the avalanche-prone headwall which leads to the North Col at 22,000 feet above Advance Base Camp.

him to lower altitudes but he died in our midst. We had to leave his body on the mountain, buried in an icy grave at 19,000 feet. It was a horrible experience and has haunted my dreams on many occasions.

After returning home, I reflected a lot on the lessons I learned and the feeling I had about my newfound passion. Very soon I was back on the road seeking new adventures. I realised that I had experienced far greater failures than not reaching the summit of Everest. My plan was to return, but first to begin my Seven Summits Challenge. A plan was hatched: McKinley first, then back to Everest. Two years later, and after extensive fundraising, BOC Gases provided sponsorship, and the dream was back on course. I was now a wiser climber and had accumulated more knowledge of high altitude mountaineering.

A memorial stone to Dr Karl Henize who died from altitude sickness during Pat Falvey's first Everest expedition.

1995 EVEREST NORTH SIDE

It takes the best part of 50 days to acclimatise your body to reach the summit of Everest and I knew it wouldn't be easy. Jon Tinker would lead the expedition again, and a number of climbers who did not reach the summit in 1993 were back on the mountain.

I met up with the rest of my team in Kathmandu. Immediately, one guy stood out from the other team members. James Allen was a young climber from Australia, full of the joys of life, with a huge positive attitude. An easy friendship developed, and during our travel to Base Camp we decided we would team up as climbing companions on Everest.

Just as on my first attempt, we were climbing Everest from the North side. The main obstacle on this side of the mountain is the final summit push to overcome the main Northeast Ridge. After this, the mountain rises slowly to the summit but is broken by three formidable barriers, known as the steps. The first step was the last place that Mallory and Irvine had been spotted before they disappeared. The second (and most dangerous) was the infamous ladder put up by the Chinese in their attempt to be the first to summit from the North. The final step was a relatively easy barrier to the upper reaches and the summit.

We moved fast and light, rushing back up to Advanced Base Camp, below the North Col. We rested for the night, and the following day traversed the steep face to Camp 1 at the North Col, before heading up to Camp 2, beneath the Northeast Ridge where Mallory and Irvine had been lost in the 1920s.

The following morning we reached High Camp at 8,200 metres, exhausted but ready for a summit bid. Two other members of our team joined us: Brigid Muir – an Australian – and Mike Smith – an Englishman, as well as Miko Valanne from Finland – a member of a team led by Russell Brice (a New Zealander living in France).

At exactly midnight we started our attempt for the summit. In freezing cold – 35 degrees below zero with a light breeze – the five of us set out. With only the beam of light from our head torches, we weaved our way along a slope punctuated by rock sentinels towards the base of the first step. Before reaching it, Brigid and Miko decided to descend. The ground up to here was easy and we knew they would have no difficulty in returning to High Camp.

Beyond the first step was a gentle ascent, traversing an easily angled slope. It felt like walking on a steep pitched roof ... except that the fall was 2,000 feet. This led to the main crux of our climb – the second step. We were making good time now, with our team down to just three, and we arrived here just as dawn was breaking at 6am.

This is the most demanding section of the climb: the 30-metre barrier of rock that holds the notorious Chinese ladder. Placed there some time in the 1970s, the ladder is still used today to break onto the upper reaches. After this, the climb gets somewhat easier to the third step, over which is the summit slope. Using words like 'easy' can be misleading, as all the dangers of high altitude and weather mean one tiny mistake can cost you your life in the thin air of the Death Zone. We made our way

from the traverse into a few tricky moves leading up a chimney-like crack, then into a gully that leads to the ladder. The ladder, which just dangles there, swayed precariously in the wind. As I ascended I wondered if I would be the climber to pull it loose from its anchor, which would see me tumbling thousands of feet down the mountain.

On James' turn, he got stuck. The ladder was incredibly unnerving, rocking in and out and swaying side to side. To get to the upper slope, James removed one of his three pairs of gloves. It was like putting his hands into liquid nitrogen, and James lost two of his fingers to frostbite for the mistake. But the worst was over; after overcoming the second step, we felt sure we would reach the summit. We made our way over the third step, and the summit slope came into view.

It felt totally surreal as we silently plodded in a trance-like state up the final 100 metres. The air had the same quiet feeling of being in a church. For a while, I had an experience where it felt as if my spirit had left my body and hovered above me. I could see myself as I slogged my way upward. In a surreal dream world, my spirit re-entered my body on the summit and my emotions ran wild.

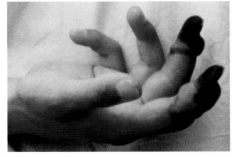

James Allen's frostbitten fingers.

Facing page: Pat Falvey at 23,500 feet with the North Col Camp behind and below him.

The North/Northeast Ridge shot below the second step and above the first step.

The dangerous second step which leads to the upper slope and the main crux of the climb at 28,000 feet.

Pat Falvey on the summit of Everest in 1995, a dream realised.

Pat Falvey at the third step in 1995.

James, Mike and I stood in awe of what was unfolding all around us. We looked at each other with eyes wide open, and were amazed at our achievement. The whole of the Himalaya unfolded around us! I felt as if I could see every mountain in the 2,000-mile Himalayan chain. This had been an amazing journey for me, which all stemmed from my depression at going broke, and my very first walks on the Kerry hills with my mentor, Val Deane. After taking in the all-encompassing view, I took my Irish tri-colour from my pocket, tied it to my ice axe and held it high in the air, roaring out, 'Yes, I have done it! I'm really standing on top of the world!' We hugged each other and took some photographs.

As I walked away from the summit, my mind was full of new ideas. Even though I had achieved my Everest, new adventures were already stimulating my mind as I descended. I knew it was time to go back to my hills in Kerry to plan what would be next.

McKINLEY

Mount McKinley / Denali

Alaska Range

Alaska, North America

6,194 metres

McKINLEY

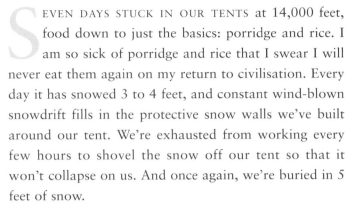

S EVEN DAYS STUCK IN OUR TENTS at 14,000 feet, food down to just the basics: porridge and rice. I am so sick of porridge and rice that I swear I will never eat them again on my return to civilisation. Every day it has snowed 3 to 4 feet, and constant wind-blown snowdrift fills in the protective snow walls we've built around our tent. We're exhausted from working every few hours to shovel the snow off our tent so that it won't collapse on us. And once again, we're buried in 5 feet of snow.

'Con, it's your turn to dig around the tent.'

'No, Falvey it's yours.'

Neither of us wants to go out in the cold.

We are on the side of Mount McKinley in June 1994, stuck in one of the typical storms that blast this mountain. Con and I are part of a nine-person Irish expedition to this peak, which is considered the coldest, most unpredictable mountain in the world. Four of us reached the summit eight days ago: Mick Murphy, Finbar Desmond, my climbing partner and tent mate Con Collins and me. But on our descent, just after we had been reunited with the team at Camp 4, a storm broke out.

MOUNT McKINLEY

Denali (The High One) was the original name for Mount McKinley, probably because it rises—almost completely isolated—from a relatively flat plane. This mountain is the highest on the North American continent, and success here just cannot to be taken for granted. My first time climbing this mountain, I was curious about why I felt worse at this lower altitude than I had at the same height on Everest. Later I came across an explanation: that because of variations in the atmosphere at the Poles, the oxygen levels decline faster which makes it feel like the equivalent of 2,000 feet higher on Denali.

McKinley from the air after take-off from Talkeetna.

Above: Camp 5 at 14,200 feet near the headwall.

Facing page –

Top: Con Collins approaching the summit in 1994.

Bottom left: Shovelling snow from around the tent at Camp 5.

Bottom right: Climbers ascending the headwall of the West Buttress.

Ascending the West Buttress Ridge towards Camp 6, the High Camp, with Mount Foraker in the background.

The climb to the summit had been spectacular. We ascended fast and furious, and after just six days we arrived at Camp 4, and had it fully stocked. Our intention was to spend four days acclimatising here before our push to the upper reaches of the mountain. However, we were issued a severe weather warning at 5pm: a big storm was approaching the mountain and would hit us in 36 hours. We had a team meeting and made a 'bold' decision to go for the summit that evening, foregoing further acclimatisation. We knew each other well as a team, and had a good idea we had the ability to pull it off. So it was decided we would take three hours to get ready and then go for it. At 8pm, in the failing light, we started for the summit.

The climb began with a 45 degree, 1,200 foot head-wall to gain the West Buttress. We then moved along a serrated and spectacular jagged ridge, weaving in and out of steep, exposed rock outcrops and pinnacles before reaching High Camp. The night was cold and beautiful as the skies turned a soft pinkish-orange colour close to midnight. At High Camp we were lucky to find a snow cave left by another team. We rested here for a few hours to boil water and eat some food. We also set up a tent in case we needed it on our return.

We then set off: Mick, Finbar, Con and I started the long, slow traverse of the sweeping ice slope to the Denali Pass. This area in particular has been the scene of accidents and deaths as tired climbers return from the summit. By the time we reached here and regrouped for a team meeting, Finbar and Mick had decided to rest. Con and I decided to continue as quickly as possible to gain the summit ridge, taking advantage of every minute of good weather. By the time we approached the ridge, we were absolutely exhausted from slogging across a flat boring area called the Football Field. However, on reaching the incline our energy levels rose with the spectacular views that were unfolding all around. Adrenaline pumping, we made our way across a narrow corniced ridge to the summit. With hugs and congratulations, we took time to admire the views from the highest point on the North American continent, taking pictures and some film footage.

Before very long we decided to move, aware of the incoming storm. On the way back between the Summit Ridge and the Football Field we met with Mick and Finbar. They congratulated us and we wished them the best, knowing that they would reach the summit – they were now only an hour away. Later that day we met back at High Camp just as the weather was about to break and rested in our tent for a few hours. Early the next morning we descended to Camp 4 with conditions worsening all the time. The team was delighted with our success.

Unloading the plane at Base Camp on the Kahiltna Glacier, 7,200 feet.

Food for the mountain. 'If I ever see rice again …'

CAMP 4, REPRISE

2006: Twelve years later, and we were back in the same camp site – Camp 4, stuck again. We had been trapped by weather here for thirteen days, in what was eventually recorded as one of the worst continuous storms to hit Denali in years. This was much longer then we had planned on being here and our food stocks had run low. Once more I was eating porridge and rice and swearing that I would never eat it again … it was like doing penance for some sin I had committed. This time, however, we made a decision to sit the storm out.

This was a return visit with Clare O'Leary and some friends on her mission to become the first Irish woman to complete the Seven Summits Challenge. Despite being stuck at Camp 4 again, I was still struck by how much I loved this mountain. It's a real expedition outing and provides everything to test mountaineering skills … although the most important skill I seemed to require here was patience – and once again, this mountain was requiring it in spades.

We were a small team, which is always nice because it's easy to manage, especially when you're a bunch of friends – we were all from Ireland, and knew each other well. As a bonus, one of our team, Ger McDonnell, was living in Anchorage, Alaska.

Ger had everything organised for us on our arrival in Alaska. He bought all the food and stored it in his girlfriend's house. We sorted all the food and the rest of our equipment, loaded it into Ger and Annie's van and headed for Talkeetna. That was my second visit to this outback town full of interesting and weird people.

For this attempt, we had to collect a permit from the National Park Office, which included a drum to carry with us. We were required to use it as a toilet, so we could carry it back off the mountain. Of course we had to draw straws as to who would take responsibility for it. They adopt the policy that we only leave footprints and no waste.

After sorting our paperwork, we went to a small airstrip just outside the town and hired two planes to fly us in onto the Kahiltna Glacier. We packed the little planes with all our gear and enjoyed one of the most spectacular small aircraft flights in the world.

We flew over the tundra aiming for the mountains through a small gap called One Shot Pass. We all cringed at what this bush pilot was attempting to do. The wings of the plane nearly touched the mountainside as we entered a new world of snow and ice. Twenty minutes later we landed at Base Camp on the Southeast fork of the Kahiltna Glacier, unpacked all our gear and began our expedition.

We loaded our sleds and headed off up the glacier, roped together for fear of falling into crevasses. The weather wasn't bad, allowing us to move straightaway up to Camp 1 at the base of an easy slope called Ski Hill. Over the following five days we made our way to Camp 2 at the Kahiltna Pass. We slept in the morning and moved only at night, to avoid melting snow bridges. In this manner we climbed through Camp 3 and finally reached Camp 4.

Building snow walls at Camp 5 in preparation for the bad weather.

RICE AND PORRIDGE ... AGAIN

Finally, on the fourteenth day of waiting at Camp 4, the winds stopped. Our merry band of Irish climbers were now running out of time – we had a flight to catch in four days! One of our team decided to abandon his summit attempt and descend – it was crucial that he did not miss the plane back to Ireland. The rest of us decided to go for it and give our best shot at reaching the summit, hoping to still make the flight. We were fully acclimatised and had stayed fit by building and repairing our snow walls daily. We retraced our steps from 1994, up the headwall, along the ridge to High Camp, only this time we did stop to sleep at Camp 5. The following morning early we headed for the summit. The views were as spectacular as I remembered. The five of us reached the summit together – John Roche from Limerick, John Dowd from Kerry, Ger McDonnell from Alaska, Clare O'Leary and myself. This was number five of Clare's Seven Summit Challenge.

I was also on my way to completing them as well, not once but twice, and now had only two to go: Mount Kosciusko in Australia and Mount Vinson in the Antarctic. On the summit Ger played the *bodrhán* and sang a song. Looking at my watch, I said, 'Right, let's go, we have a flight to catch'.

It was a hard push to Base Camp. It took us thirty-six hours non-stop, resting only for food, drink and a short nap at each camp site. Stripping our gear from the camps as we went, we collected our garbage, still hauling the two sealed buckets of our human waste. Our sleds and backpacks were full to the brim as we crossed the Kahiltna Glacier to Base Camp.

With no time to waste, we packed up Ger and Annie's van again and headed for our scheduled flight back to Ireland out of Anchorage. We had reached the summit and made our flight with only twenty minutes to spare!

Thirty-six hours later, exhausted from my fast exit from McKinley, I was on another flight with a group of Irish climbers headed to Kilimanjaro in Africa.

Facing page –
Top: Denali Summit Ridge.
Bottom: Climbers on the Kahiltna Glacier with sleds in tow.

At the summit in 2005, left to right:
Pat Falvey, John Dowd, Clare O'Leary, Ger McDonnell and John Roche.

KILIMANJARO

Tanzania, Africa

5,895 metres

I HAVE OFTEN BEEN ASKED what is my favourite place in the world, and I always answer that there are two: one is Nepal, and the other is Africa. Africa is a truly amazing continent, from Morocco in the north, to Tanzania where Mount Kilimanjaro sits, to the comfort and sandy beaches on the island of Zanzibar, the sophistication of Cape Town.

I have climbed to the lofty peak of Kilimanjaro at least twenty times. It is one of the few mountains where I have the opportunity to show people with no prior training what it's like to climb a high altitude mountain. It is made even more unique by the five different climate zones on the way to the summit. It always blows me away to stand there on the icy peak, silent as the sun rises, its great fiery head glowing above the clouds in the African sky ... but catch it while you can. I have seen many changes due to global warming, but none so plainly visible as the receding glacier on the summit of Kilimanjaro. Each year it shocks me to see the increasing absence of snow and ice on this peak.

Kilimanjaro is made even more exciting because of the colourful people that surround it, including the Masai and the Bantu tribes. Over the years I have made many friends with local people. For me, Africa is not just about climbing Kilimanjaro – the highest mountain on the continent. It is enhanced by the sight and colour of the people that surround it, and its wildlife. A stunning variety of animals inhabit the slopes of this mountain, including hornbills, monkeys, antelope and hyrax. We usually go on safari to Ngorongoro Crater to view the 'Big 5' in their native habitat: rhino, leopard, buffalo, lion and elephant, and to Lake Manyara for its abundance of wild life and the tree-climbing lions. Travelling on through the plains of the Serengeti, we experience the Rift Valley – one of the great wonders of the world, which stretches from the Middle East, down through Africa and Mozambique. Often, the warm sands and relaxation found on the tropical island of Zanzibar help us unwind at the end of our journey.

MOUNT KILIMANJARO

Kilimanjaro, formerly Kaiser-Wilhelm-Spitze, is an inactive stratovolcano in north-eastern Tanzania. Although it does not have the highest elevation, Kilimanjaro is the tallest free-standing mountain rise in the world, rising 4,600 metres (15,000 ft) from its base, and includes the highest peak in Africa at 5,895 metres (19,340 ft), providing a dramatic view from the surrounding plains.

Glacier remnants near the summit at the top of the Mashame/Arrow Glacier route.

Facing page: Kilimanjaro aerial view showing the crater cone, the top of the Mashame/Arrow Glacier route, the summit, the Baraffo descent route and Gilman's Point/Marangu route.

Top: Crater safari in Ngorongoro.

Bottom: Porters weighing the gear bags.

Top: Gerry Walsh and a young villager.

Middle: Lioness and cubs dining.

Bottom: Young Masai farm workers on the foothills of Kilimanjaro.

THE MASAI

Over 250,000 Masai live in Kenya and Tanzania. They are one of the few tribes left in Africa that still endeavour to live their traditional way of life. They have a great dependence on cattle, following their herds across the plains in search of pastures. It's sad that, due to land restrictions, their movements are more controlled and the governments of Kenya and Tanzania are now encouraging them to settle and abandon their nomadic ways.

When visiting Masai villages on the edge of the great Ngorongoro Crater, we are often treated to a display of their ritual dance. The Masai warriors are tall and intimidating, standing proud. Their unusual dance – hopping more than 4 feet in the air, singing in throbbing drones, humming like a revving engine – fascinates me every time. The pitch climbs higher and higher as they sing their wordless tunes. A final shrill high note signals the end of the song, and the dancing begins. We are always astounded as we watch them spring effortlessly into the air, the ground acting as a trampoline, with each warrior competing to out-jump the others.

Masai performing their dance.

Top: A Masai infant in its mother's sling.
Middle: Sunset on the plain.
Bottom: An elderly Masai.

Camping on the rocky, lunar landscape of the higher slopes.

Africa really impressed me the first time I visited in 1996, and within twelve months I was back there again, bringing a group on a fundraising mission. We were on a high, so excited that we had raised €250,000 for their cause. But this could not outshine the fact that my son Brian, who was on his break year, accompanied us.

Arriving in Nairobi in the middle of the night can be a frightening experience for those who have not encountered the hustle of an African city. Filled with prostitutes and pimps, around every corner the peering, glazed eyes of street gangs are focused on you. It is easy – and probably wise – to become paranoid in a city that has a reputation for violence, wondering if you are going to be attacked and robbed.

Our group's most immediate desire was to get out of this city as quickly as possible. The following day we left the bustle and clutter of Nairobi and made our way to the border town of Manang, heading across the savannah to Kilimanjaro.

As the largest freestanding mountain in the world, what makes this mountain so unusual and exciting to climb is the cross section of terrain and natural environments through which you pass. The journey from the base in the African plains to the glaciated top brings you through five very different and distinct ecological zones. No matter how many times I travel here, I am always elated as I pass through the gates of the Kilimanjaro National Park. From here we walk through the coffee, maize and banana plantations and the villages of the vibrant, colourful Chaga people.

There are eleven different routes to Kilimanjaro's summit, Uhuru Peak. Having had the opportunity to climb on most, my two favourite routes are the Coca-Cola Route and the Whiskey Route. The names are not indicative of the effort needed to summit. Instead, they suggest the amount of comfort that exists on either route. On the so-called Coca-Cola route, you have the opportunity to stay in comfortable, basic huts. Although I love the Marango, or Coca-Cola Route for its comfort, my own preference is the Machame, Arrow Glacier/ Barafu Route, also known as the Whiskey Route, because it gives more of a mountain experience, camping out under the stars.

On this particular trip, with my son and the fundraisers, we took the Whiskey Route. We left the savannah with its wide plains, passing up through the fertile coffee plantations. Later, we worked our way higher on the mountain under the vibrant green canopy of a rainforest jungle, sighting unusual birds and animals and hearing many more. From here we emerged from the dense foliage into high alpine meadows, the sudden change of which was almost a shock. Climbing higher, we ventured onto the barren, rocky lunar moonscape of the upper slopes. Air was getting thin here, and I checked the team to make sure nobody was suffering from the altitude. Luckily, everybody was doing well.

Finally we reached the summit plateau with its permanent glaciers. It seemed almost unbelievable to be crunching through snow while gazing down over Africa. Just five days after starting, here we were looking at one of the greatest nature shows on earth. Standing on the summit we watched the sun rise over the Indian Ocean and African plains, illuminating the icy roof of Africa.

A porter at sunrise.

A porter on the higher slopes.

On the summit plateau.

On the summit with Joe O'Leary (left) and my son Brian.

Over the years I have accompanied many people to Kilimanjaro. Often those who join me here have little or no mountain climbing experience, but many have gone on to climb bigger and more technical peaks, including Mount Everest, and others in the Seven Summits series. It is not unusual for me to bring entire families up this mountain together, from grandparents to grandchildren. This time I was especially honoured to share the experience with my own son. I have never known anyone who was not moved by the impressions that Africa leaves on you, especially the summit of Kilimanjaro. I can easily call this my favourite mountain in the world.

ELBRUS

Caucasus Range

Russia

5,642 metres

ELBRUS

CHECHNYA

I COULD SEE A HEAVILY ARMED CHECKPOINT up ahead, a convoy of tanks and about 50 soldiers, all carrying machine guns and ready for action. It was March 1996, and my first visit to the Caucasus. The military were everywhere, the war in Chechnya was at its peak – it was the time Groznyy was being bombarded, and over 100,000 people had lost their lives in two war-torn years. I knew we would be within 150 miles of the war front, and I was concerned for the safety of our expedition. We were making our way to our destination in Terskol, which would act as our Base Camp in a tiny village at the head of the Baksan Valley, in the central Caucasus.

THE VOLATILE CAUCASUS

The Caucasus mountains stretch 550 miles from the Black Sea to the Caspian Sea. They form the physical barrier dividing Europe and Asia, although the whole mountain range lies entirely within the former Soviet Union. During my first few visits, this area was one of the most politically unstable in the world, with 50 different ethnic groups battling for independence from repressive regimes. We were here to do a winter ascent on Mount Elbrus, in the peaceful region of Kabardino-Balkaria.

MOUNT ELBRUS, located in the western Caucasus mountains, in Kabardino-Balkaria and Karachay-Cherkessia, Russia, near the border of Georgia. A stratovolcano that has lain dormant for about 2,000 years, it is the highest mountain in the Caucasus. Mount Elbrus (west summit) stands at 5,642 m (18,510 ft) and can be considered to be the highest mountain in Europe. The east summit is slightly lower: 5,621 metres (18,442 feet).

The twin cones of Elbrus from the valley.

MOUNT ELBRUS

The highest and most glaciated section of the Caucasus is the central region, which includes Mount Elbrus – the highest mountain in Europe. Elbrus is a popular twin-peaked dome mountain, and involves a straightforward glacier climb to its summit. The main hazards are high altitude and poor weather, and in 1999, the bureaucratic personnel stationed in this highly corrupt area.

My climbing partner, George, was a skinny, gregarious, Vodka-drinking Russian that I had become friends with on Everest. Approaching the military blockade, George turned to me and in his inimitable English said, 'Just give me 10,000 rubles and don't say nothing – just nod and follow my lead.'

'OK, George.' This was the equivalent of just two dollars at the time. George gave the money to the taxi driver, who calmly rolled down the window and chatted with the soldier. I watched the taxi driver slide the 10,000 rubles into his hand. We were then ushered by two machine-gun carrying soldiers through a series of tanks. We encountered a further two checkpoints like this before we completed our 150km trip to Terskol.

I have returned to the region eight times to climb this mountain, and much has changed. Many of the more remarkable changes occurred after the bombing in 2004 of a school in Beslan, North Ossetia, when a group of Pro-Chechen warlord gangs held 1,200 school children and adults hostage. A bloodbath ensued, with 344 civilians dying in a stand-off, including 186 children.

As a result of this horrific event, ordinary people throughout the region revolted. Militias that once ruled the people by fear have disappeared and an uneasy peace now exists.

One of the many Russian armoured personnel carriers.

Elbrus from a distance.

ADVENTURE ON THE MOUNTAIN

Once in the mountains anything can happen. Reinhold Messner, one of the world's most famous mountaineers, said, 'Mountains are not fair or unfair. They are dangerous'. I have stood on the summit of this mountain in a tee-shirt, and I have battled on the same mountain at the same time of year in white-out conditions with temperatures of -40 degrees Celsius. The most important lesson I have learned from Elbrus is never, ever underestimate this or any other mountain. This type of mountain is particularly deceiving – it looks easy, and seems easy, even as far as High Camp.

A NIGHT IN A TIN CAN

It's easy to assume that accidents on a mountain will happen due to weather conditions, avalanches, on the glaciers or performing dangerous mountain activities. But this is not always the case, as I was reminded on my second visit to Elbrus.

At High Camp on Elbrus, climbers traditionally used a hut that was built in 1938–39. The hut had the capacity to shelter 200 climbers, built by the Russians to train their armies in polar and mountain warfare over the years. In the recent past it had become a base for climbers making a summit attempt on Europe's highest mountain. I would describe it as an ugly three-storey tin can. Another description I read once called it, 'a beautiful three-storey aluminium-clad hotel'. I remember George and I being the only climbers there on my first attempt at Elbrus in winter.

View of Ushpa Peak from Elbrus.

Approaching the Priut hut in 1991.

DANGER WHEN WE LEAST EXPECTED IT

Two years after our first expedition on the mountain I was back again with George and a group of Irish climbers. We had booked places in the hut for three nights during our ascent of Elbrus. All the team were in high spirits having acclimatised on our training peak – an icy mountain called Kumachi in the Adsul valley, rising on the edge of Georgia. Trekking through the beautiful alpine meadows of Cheget, and looking across the valley to Elbrus, we confidently approached the hut.

We had a hard slog up the mountain, carrying full packs from our last camping site at Krugozor, a cable car station on the slopes of Elbrus, built for Russian skiers. Following the cable car line, we walked from here up a 1,220 metre rise to the hut. Reaching The Mir Station, the highest stop for the cable car, we continued up the mountain, trudging slowly along a rocky road. Passing the Garabashi Barrels, another camp site, our thoughts were fixed upon the comfort of our tin can higher on the mountain and we continued up a snowy incline to the Priut Hut.

With a perfect three-day weather forecast, we were confident everyone had it in them to summit, having successfully acclimatised in the surrounding valleys.

Climbing higher on Mount Elbrus, the views were spectacular. We stopped every few minutes, admiring the surrounding Caucasus as we approached the Priut Hut.

We took it easy, as we were getting tired from ascending over 1,000 metres. We knew we had all evening to get there. We could see our eventual target ahead: the massive twin peaks of Elbrus, shooting sky-wards. Everyone was inquisitive about the route to finish the final climb. 'The hardest section is ahead, up to those rocks,' I pointed 'and then we'll ascend a long, sweeping traverse between the twin peaks. The summit is on the left – the higher of the two peaks by only twenty metres.'

The team was excited to see the summit so close. 'Right lads, let's move. A few more minutes and we can cook up dinner.'

At that moment, four Russians ran toward us, roaring in alarm, 'Fire, fire, fire!' In split seconds I heard the crack of broken glass, and people began running down towards us to get away from the building. Four more people ran out the main door with bellows of smoke following them. All I could hope was that nobody was caught inside.

There was panic everywhere, and it took a while to find out what had happened. A Russian climber was boiling water in the main dining area over a stove, and had poured a drum of white fuel into a pan to cook with, thinking it was water. When a few drops of the white fuel hit the open flames and flared, the climber threw more white fuel on the fire, still thinking it was water. He was killed in the ensuing fire.

We were all in shock. George and Joe O'Leary, my Irish climbing partner, gathered our team together and decided to head back down to the Garabashi Barrels. Knowing that the fire would displace over 200 climbers, we decided Joe would bring the team back down to the lower campsite to secure a place for the team to stay the night. George and I would stay to see if we could help. The fire was blazing out of control, and there was nothing to fight it with.

Luckily, we got one of the Barrels. It would accommodate all twelve climbers if we squeezed in, but we would have to check out the following day, because they were already booked. This meant our only option was to make a go for the summit that night. Now, what would have been an easy summit became a hard task. We would have to ascend again from the Barrels at 3,800 metres all the way to the summit if we were to stand any chance at all. We decided to go for it, and at two in the morning we made an unscheduled attempt on the summit. Due to fatigue and altitude sickness, and after a great try by all, only six of our climbers got to the summit. Exhausted, we returned to the Barrels at 3pm the following day, and descended the mountain by chair-lift and cable car.

When we finally reached the safety of the valley we felt lucky to be alive. The dorm we had booked in the Priut Hut was on the third floor, and we pondered over what would have happened if we had reached our destination even one hour earlier.

The Priut Hut is engulfed in fire in 1998.

Injured being helped down from the Priut Hut.

The Barrels, constructed like huge oil tanks, provide accommodation for skiers and climbers.

Top: Acclimatising in the valleys around Terskol.

Middle: A climber enjoying the rich botany of the area.

Bottom: Local flora.

Facing page: The col between the twin peaks of Elbrus.

A rescue helicopter near the slopes of Elbrus.

Returning from the summit.

ACONCAGUA

Argentina

Andes Range

6,962 metres

Arriving in Mendoza, Argentina, a huge billboard dominates the roadside on the way from the airport. It urges the passer by to 'Come to Mendoza', further proclaiming that the Mendoza region has the most beautiful women and the best wines in the world. I've been to Mendoza eight times and I can confirm the truthfulness of Argentinean advertising. More than that, the city – with over a million residents – is an energetic and cosmopolitan place. Wide, tree-lined leafy boulevards with cafés and wine bars offer outdoor seating, and there is no nicer way to spend the afternoon than sipping coffee or beer, soaking up the sun and watching the world go by.

But for me, the interest here is in climbing. Less than four hours from this bustling city is Aconcagua – the highest mountain on the South American continent. The history of this mountain is steeped in the ancient culture of the Andes. For the Incas, Aconcagua was a temple. Many sacred items have been found, including a mummy, which confirms the importance this 'Stone Sentry' had for the original inhabitants.

Before my first adventure, climbing Aconcagua in 1995 for my Seven Summits Challenge, I had been told it was a 'slag heap' of a mountain. After scaling its heights, I couldn't disagree more. This is a great mountain to climb, and I have come to love travelling to this area.

If you are looking for the experience of an expedition mountain, Aconcagua is an ideal place to start. It sits on the border of Argentina and Chile, and is not only the highest peak in South America, but also the highest mountain in the world outside of the Himalaya in Asia. For those completing the Seven Summits Challenge, it's important as the continental high point. As training for the higher Himalayan peaks, it provides an opportunity for climbers to experience an expedition on a high-altitude mountain.

One of my favourite aspects of climbing Aconcagua is the journey to Base Camp through the desert landscape with the Gaucho muleteers. They ride in on horseback, herding pack mules through the barren and dusty valleys. Following on foot with our packs, we travel through this arid land of hardly any vegetation alongside gushing rivers of snow melt. To cross these rivers, we're taken in turn on horseback, sometimes sinking up to our haunches in water. Because only camp provisions are carried on the mules, our own packs are heavy, and the journey is not always easy.

Boulevard cafés in Mendoza.

ACONCAGUA

Cerro Aconcagua is the highest mountain in the Americas. It is located in the Andes mountain range, in the Argentine province of Mendoza. The summit is located about 5 kilometres from San Juan Province and 15 kilometres from the international border with Chile. It lies 112km west by north of the city of Mendoza. Aconcagua is the highest peak in both the Western and Southern Hemispheres, as well as the highest outside of Asia. It is one of the Seven Summits.

Facing page: Aconcagua viewed from the Vacas Valley showing the Polish Glacier.

Approaching Base Camp from Vacas Valley Route.

CAMPFIRES AND ASADO

Stopping to make camp at night, we gather around fires where the famous Argentinean beef, asado, is prepared. The beef is superb, crackling and sizzling on the hot grills, as the smell of roasting meat fills the air. Gathered under the stars around the campfire, lively music sessions often last into the night. Later, camping under the open skies by firelight quiets the soul.

THE STONE SENTINEL

It takes fifteen to eighteen days to tackle this mountain via the most popular routes of the Vacas or Horcones Valleys. Otherwise, there is a risk of developing acute mountain sickness. Of all the mountains I climb, Aconcagua is the most misleading in many respects. Over the years I have seen climbers who have pushed themselves to the limit on this mountain, and never return to tell the tale.

Despite its reputation as a non-technical high altitude climb, less than one-third of the thousands of climbers who attempt Aconcagua each year actually succeed. Many succumb to the cruel effects of the *viento blanco*, or white wind, which rages at over 100 miles per hour. Others suffer from altitude sickness, to be evacuated by helicopter or carried down on a mule. This is a mountain on which conditions change from year to year. I have been here when it was mild, with very low rivers, and have even reached the summit in a T-shirt! Other times, I've needed crampons, an ice axe and full polar gear to summit. So, you never know.

Top: View of Aconcagua from Camp 2 in the Vacas Valley.

Bottom: Gaucho muleteers cooking a barbecue of roast beef or 'asado'.

Bad weather near the Polish Glacier.

On one occasion, I had just reached the peak with my climbing partner, and we were celebrating our achievement. It was New Year's Eve, and this year, the peak was icy and covered with snow. Earlier in the week we spent Christmas at Camp 1, in our tents to keep from freezing in the newly-fallen snow. It happens that I'm almost always away at Christmas, wondering what it would be like to just stay at home in front of a blazing fire some year!

Originally, we planned to ascend the mountain over the Polish Glacier, but due to bad weather and avalanche risk, we had to alter our plans. On the way we befriended some American climbers who decided when we changed plans to travel with us. We traversed the mountain to another campsite called White Rocks, making this our base for the final push.

A TROUBLED START TO THE NEW YEAR

The next day we began our summit bid directly from White Rocks. The others in our camp were not sure they would continue, some suffering from the altitude and not feeling well. Our ascent took us over the desolate upper slopes of the mountain. I am always struck by the contrast between the landscape high on the mountain compared to that of Base Camp and Camp 1. When passing through this lower section you'll find the unusual ice formations called penitentes. They look as though they are permanent features in the landscape, but they are formed by the sun melting snow on the slope. Some years, the entire slope is bristling with these mini-peaks, and other years they're not here at all. Up this high, there is little to capture our interest, and we focus only on advancing up the mountain. After some hours of climbing, we reached the summit, and taking in the views, considered the new year ahead.

As we sat enjoying the view, one of the Americans appeared in the distance. Earlier he had been unsure whether he would go for the summit, but he was now staggering toward us, gasping for breath. Suffering badly from altitude sickness, he fell to his knees. Con Collins and I looked at each other, and I knew we were thinking the same thing. Though Eugene was not part of our expedition we had become friends while climbing the mountain and felt a responsibility to ensure his safe return. Even if we didn't know him at all, we would have followed an unwritten code of practice that says you come to the aid of a fellow climber. Altitude sickness can happen to anybody and I'd like to think that my fellow climbers would help me if I were suffering.

We let Eugene rest for about ten minutes and then suggested that we get going, because the longer he stayed up here the worse he'd get. We departed, hoping to descend speedily to our High Camp at White Rocks. Once we got there we would celebrate New Year's Eve with a few drops of Irish whiskey saved for the occasion. Our progress was slow as we retraced our steps through the deep snow, across the Cresta Del Guanaco Ridge to the col dividing the main summit from the bottom South Summit.

Eugene was now very unsteady on his feet and staggered like a drunken man. We understood there was no way he would be able to descend on his own, and that very shortly he might not be able to walk. As we descended we had to negotiate a number of small rock steps, and on one of these Eugene leaned forward and tumbled, somersaulting over me, completely out of control.

As he fell to the ground I managed to jump on him, and with my ice axe I arrested our downward slide. Eugene could only lie there, unable to help himself in any way. As we lifted him to a seated position we considered our situation. The regular afternoon blizzard was now in full force, and we needed to act fast. There was no way the two of us were going to be able to help Eugene down safely in this state. We decided that I would go on for help. At this point the stricken climber was in severe shock. As quickly as I could I took off down the mountain to raise a rescue.

Top: Pat Falvey struggles through the Penitentes in 1994.
Bottom: View towards the summit with the Polish Glacier to the left.

Eventually I reached Eugene's climbing partners, who joined me in descending further to Camp Berlin and radioing for help. I then turned back up the trail to Con and Eugene. In the meantime, a guide named Catherine, who was guiding four Spaniards, passed Con on her descent from the summit. Catherine offered their assistance. To her annoyance the Spaniards declined to help. Luckily, two Swiss climbers we had met earlier on the mountain, Chris and Brono, were descending and offered to help. Catherine stayed and sent the Spaniards down on their own.

Fearful for Eugene's life, they improvised a plan that would get him lower on the mountain, using what resources they had. Cutting the straps from their ice axes, they attached them to Eugene's rucksack, making an improvised toboggan, and bundled the near-lifeless Eugene into it. For the 300 metres of slope left, Eugene slid down the mountainside. At this point the group reached a horizontal traverse of the mountain to the northeast. Thinking fast, they strapped two ski poles to the rucksack and, as if dragging a sled, they pulled and shoved Eugene to the safety of the derelict broken shelter at the Independencia Refuge.

Completely exhausted, Catherine, Chris, Brono and Con rested. It was here that I met up with them. Shortly, to everyone's amazement, Eugene started to come around – the almost 400-metre descent had relieved some of his symptoms. After a brief period he declared he would be able to descend to High Camp. It was now 7.30pm and believing that Eugene would be okay, Catherine and the two Swiss lads headed down to Berlin camp while Con, Eugene and I continued to our campsite at White Rocks, sending Catherine with a message to cancel our request for help.

In the middle of the night, Eugene awoke in a bad state again. We knew the only thing to do was descend further, and immediately. Eugene was like the living dead, and we had to put on his clothes and boots while he flopped around like a limp rag doll. For the next twelve hours we dragged and pulled him through the lower camps, finally reaching Base Camp Argentine in the Vacas Valley. By the time we arrived, Eugene was feeling better again, and we finally managed to get some sleep.

EUGENE LIVES TO TELL HIS STORY

In recent years I have heard of another climber who got into the same situation as Eugene, but wasn't as lucky. He had climbed to the summit late in the day, on his own. Suffering from oedema, he simply didn't have the energy to get back down safely. Without a climbing partner or others on the summit, there was nobody to encourage him or assist him in his descent. The rescue team evacuated his body.

Luckily for Eugene, upon waking the next day and descending further, he made a full recovery. He certainly left this unpredictable mountain with an interesting story to tell back home in California! Con and I were just glad to see him alive and well. It was, indeed, a happy new year.

Facing page: Climbing the Canalleta.

Another successful group led by Pat Falvey to the summit.

Above: View towards the summit from above White Rocks.

Left: The return journey.

Facing page:
Looking down on Berlin Camp.

IRIAN JAYA

Irian Jaya / West Papua

Indonesia

H E STOOD THERE PROUDLY AND CRIED, in an angry voice, 'We were once free and now look at us. What have we done wrong Has God forsaken us. All we did was welcome strangers with open arms, and now they strip us of our lands, kill our traditions. They herd us like cattle from our homes into villages while they cut down our forest and rape the land of its minerals. They poison our rivers and destroy our homes.'

He went on to explain that he never thought his people 'would be displaced and treated like this, no better than dogs on the street'. He felt no one cared that thousands of his people had been killed in their struggle for basic human rights: 'We were a simple people who had no disagreement with the rest of the world. Now we are prisoners in our own land, displaced and dejected.'

Justinius Toko Darby spoke with passion. As the voice of his people, he was fighting for a cause that fell on deaf ears. Justinius was one of the few among his people who had been educated by Catholic missionaries in the coastal city of Jayapura, the capital of West Papua. Being the son of a powerful Dani Chief, missionaries believed this strategic education would be a way of capturing the souls of the Neolithic warriors living deep in the jungle.

Education had served him well. We were honoured to be able to hear the views of someone living in the remote tropical region of West Papua.

Facing page: The dense rainforest of Irian Jaya.

Right: Justinius.

IRIAN JAYA / WEST PAPUA

West Papua (Indonesian: Papua Barat; formerly West Irian Jaya or Irian Jaya Barat) is a province of Indonesia on the western end of the island of New Guinea. It covers the Bird's Head (or Doberai) Peninsula and surrounding islands.

The province has a population of approximately 800,000, making it one of the least populous of all Indonesian provinces. The capital of West Papua is in Manokwari.

The province changed its name to West Papua in February 2007. The new name applied from 7 February 2007, but a plenary session of the provincial legislative council is required to legalise the name, and the government needs to then issue a regulation.

Near the summit of Mount Cook.

Trikola Peak.

I was on the final leg of my Southern Hemisphere Expedition. After completing an Antarctic expedition in February 1997, I had been joined in New Zealand by my friends Con Moriarty, Gene Tagney and Mike Shea, all from County Kerry. We climbed to the summit of Mount Cook in New Zealand and Kosciuszko in Australia, which were the final peaks in my Seven Summits Challenge. As a result of my expeditions, I was becoming more fascinated by world cultures. Now, arriving on West Papua New Guinea, we intended to climb the Carstensz Pyramid.

West Papua lies between the continents of Australia and Asia and is considered the second-largest island in the world. I was especially excited about travelling here

because it was still so remote. I knew that there were still tribes here living in much the same way as they had for thousands of years, and this fascinated me.

Expeditions are about adventure, and we were having one! Our trip to Papua New Guinea provided all sorts of adventures, from the risk of being thrown in prison by the Indonesian army, to our uneasiness about whether our host would set us up for a kidnapping or not. We were somewhat nervous, being aware that a group of students from Europe had been kidnapped in 1995. Two hostages died during the rescue operation.

A few weeks earlier we had arrived in Jakarta to find that our permit to enter the interior of the island had been cancelled. Although we were really disappointed,

Pat Falvey with some Dani tribesmen.

Young children trek with Con Moriarty.

we weren't ready to give up, and spent the next seven days in a humid, smoggy city going from one department to the next – tourism, defence, foreign affairs and every type of official we could find to help us reinstate our permit. We weren't successful.

It was fortunate that while travelling in Bali on the way here from Australia, I had befriended a high-ranking official in the legal office of the Indonesian Department for Justice. Mohamed was trying to move mountains for us. He gave freely of his time and expertise in dealing with bureaucratic officials and at the start was hopeful. However, every time we thought we had a breakthrough the people involved backed off. Our issue was clearly considered a bit of a 'hot potato' by the Indonesians.

Most feared they would get into trouble if they helped us. Their advice to us was: stay away and go home. Even Mohamed feared for our safety. West Papua was making big news on international television due to the fight with the OPM, or *Free Papua Movement* – who were regarded as brutal guerrillas.

Eventually Mohamed was able to book a flight for us to the coastal city Jayapura, 'But you are wasting your time,' he warned us, 'this is as far as you will get'. Before we left, he wrote an official looking letter and placed it in an envelope. 'I have made friends with you all,' he said, 'and if you should find yourself in trouble with officials or the army, please give them this.'

Dani tribesmen in Wamena.

Top: The marketplace in Wamena.
Above: Dani people preparing for a war dance.

During these days of struggling to obtain a permit, we had been phoning friends and colleagues around the world to see if anyone had contacts in Jayapura. It turned out that a Russian friend I had met on my first trip to the Caucasus was an historian and anthropologist from Ossetia. He had a contact in Jayapura who might help us. This was Justinius, and upon arrival in Jayapura we tracked him down.

It always seems to me that just as you are about to give up, if you keep trying a new door opens. We introduced ourselves to Justinius and told him our reasons for being there. He was highly impressed, not because of our climbing objectives but because we had come from Ireland and had expressed an interest in learning about his people and their way of life. He knew all about Ireland and of our stance on East Timor, as well as our record of fighting for human rights around the world. 'You Irish are good people,' he said, and in the same breath, asked if we were freedom fighters and members of the IRA. 'No,' we answered.

The following day he organised a flight to Wamena, a small city in the jungle. We were surprised that after struggling for seven days in Jakarta trying to gain a permit, Justinius could arrange a flight the very next day. Of course, he explained the difficulty and the danger of entering what he called hostile territory. 'You do not have to worry about my people – I will make sure of that, but I do not know how we will get you to Illaga,' the base from which to leave for Carstensz Pyramid.

We boarded the plane and flew nearly 300km over impenetrable rain forest without a road in sight. Wamena, built by the Indonesians, was a city in the centre of the jungle complete with streets, shops, hotels, and markets. It was a large construction site with trucks, bulldozers, JCBs and every form of earth-moving machinery. It also had a heavy military presence. After having our papers thoroughly checked, we went to our hotel. It all seemed fairly straightforward and I was starting to wonder what all the hassle was about in Jakarta.

The next day we were asked to be ready to board a small aircraft that would take us to Illaga in a few days' time. In the meantime, we explored Wamena. This town reminded me of a film set. With no road in and no road out, the Indonesians flew everything there, including earth-moving machinery! The idea was to bulldoze a road to traverse the island and gain access to the forest and mountainous areas, which hold the greatest reserves of gold and copper in the world. The other major benefit of providing a road into this dense rain forest area was logging, and permits had already been issued to multi-national logging companies.

To occupy this area, the Indonesian government settled 250,000 Indonesians from overpopulated regions. Setting them up with businesses, they were given rights to the lands of the indigenous people. Naturally, this caused conflict, so they also provided a heavy army presence to protect these newcomers. The military was strict and had vast powers. The law stipulated, for example, that anyone raising a West Papua flag or causing a disturbance was to be shot on sight. Without ever leaving Wamena I could see why Justinius was so angry.

Visiting the shops and markets of Wamena, it became very evident that these displaced tribal people – who such a short time ago knew freedom as hunters, gatherers and trappers – were now living in an almost trance-like state. This environment was completely alien to them.

Dani tribesman with mummified ancestor.

Just as we were about to fly to Illaga a change of plan occurred: the officials who had been bribed to allow our flight were now too afraid of being found out. The plane for our departure was cancelled so Justinius hatched a second plan: to the west of Wamena was another mountain we could climb called Trikola – the second highest on the island.

A group of Dani porters, some of them naked apart from their penis gourds, agreed to take us through the dense rain forest so we could try to climb Trikola. Our head porter, Iso, was a very religious person. At every meal he would have all the porters say their prayers – *Catholic* prayers.

For five days we pushed our way through an amazing forest and lived amongst the indigenous people who eked a subsistence living from the land. We made our way from village to village through the thick forest, always on alert and aware of the fact that our enemy was now the military. We also had to worry about spies employed by the army who would readily inform on their own people.

Passing through a village just a few days away from our Base Camp, we were confronted by a chief who had taken offence to us crossing his land. The unusual thing about this chief was that he was wearing a mock police uniform, emblazoned with his title: 'Chief'. He seemed to feel this fake uniform elevated him in stature and authority. We became concerned when he demanded money for our trespassing. After much negotiating, Iso came to a settlement with him. After this incident, a mood of caution prevailed, for they feared he may have been a spy and that he would inform the army of our whereabouts. Still, the porters were great fun, and every night we'd sing their local songs as well as songs from Ireland.

Trikola was a beautiful, jagged limestone peak in open countryside. Unfortunately we didn't get to summit as we were forced to urgently return to the cover of the jungle. Our spotters had come across a convoy of soldiers who had been dropped in by helicopter, and they feared we would be discovered.

We made our way back to Wamena, just as Con, Mike and Gene's time had run out – pressures at home demanded their return. I had some extra time and wanted to stay. I was intrigued with the place and wanted to find out more about the Dani. Meeting Justinius on our return, he agreed to bring me to see some of his other friends who were chiefs in the neighbouring villages, and to visit a few of the local schools. He also agreed to fill me in more on the traditions and cultures of his people. I didn't feel I could turn such an opportunity down.

A few days later we were deep in the jungle again, visiting the villages of the Dani. I was amazed to be welcomed with open arms, and not once was I concerned about my safety. Over roaring open fires in the evening I asked hundreds of questions of Justinius.

Justinius told me the story of how his people settled in these lands around the Baliam valley. 'God left us in the jungle. We were white skinned then. But the sun was so strong that it burned our bodies, so we basked in mud to protect ourselves, and took refuge in caves that God provided. In the caves, children were born black to protect them from the sun, and when they grew up they left the caves and set up home elsewhere.' When they returned many years later their parents were gone. 'God had been merciful and took them somewhere else.'

'The Dani then became hunters, trappers and warriors, and this is how we lived. We fought amongst each other with bow and arrow. Our customs included cannibalism. When we killed a powerful chief, we would eat his brain. By doing so we felt we devoured his power, and that it would make us stronger.' They would also use some of the bones of those eaten to make knives and spears.

Justinius went on to explain that in 1938, when an American exploration team led by researcher Richard Archibald came to the Baliam valley, the people thought these white westerners were their gods and ancestors coming back to visit, and welcomed them with open arms. At that time, this was still uncharted territory, and the expedition reported widely of their exciting find. However, it was not until many years later that the white man returned. This time, it was missionaries, coming to convert the so-called heathens. Again, these white men were welcomed with open arms. Both Catholic and Protestant missionaries then arrived, and set up competing churches. Justinius, who had been raised by missionaries, became a Catholic. He was now a lay preacher, he told me – so I found it particularly amusing when he told me about his three wives!

A Dani tribesman turning a cooking pig.

Dani woman with mutilated fingers.

Sitting in the village.

The economy amongst the Dani tribe seemed to be centred on bartering, and the valued currency was swine. The more pigs you had, the wealthier you were. Pigs were especially used as dowries for tribal women. A well-off chief with lots of pigs could have many wives, since he could afford the dowry. When I asked him how many pigs for a wife, he told me a good wife would cost ten pigs. Wives could even be seen as investments, as every daughter conceived could eventually be married off in exchange for ten pigs. I asked, then, how they felt about male children, and it was explained that boys grew up to be warriors to make the tribe stronger.

On my travels around the different villages, I noticed that quite a few of the women had lost the top section of many of their fingers. I asked why, and Justinius translated the explanation:

'This is the way we traditionally demonstrate our sorrow and it is necessary for calming the spirits. One month after a member of the tribe dies, we have a ritual.' He went on to explain that up to three village women, from the age of twelve, would lose the top of one or two fingers when a close family member – especially men – died. I cringed as he detailed what seemed like a cruel ritual. The women with the missing fingers, however, just smiled and shrugged, giggling at the attention.

The following day we had a celebration for my leaving. I was presented with two of my own personal penis gourds. I'm still unsure as to what I should do with them, as they're not the kind of thing you'd nip down to the shop wearing! They also gave me a gift of a shinbone that had been carved into a knife. I accepted gracefully.

Eventually I returned to my hotel in Wamena. Justinius had organised my return flight to Jayapura. He didn't want to stay with me here as he felt it would be too dangerous for him. He decided instead to meet me back in Jayapura. On registering at the hotel, my return was reported to the army, although I didn't know it at the time.

Shortly afterwards, I saw a group of soldiers approach my hotel. Fully armed, they 'requested' my presence. The captain came into the bar and questioned me rigorously about where I had been, and with whom, in a lengthy interrogation. Unable to give any satisfactory answers, I was frankly concerned that I was going to be killed. I had one last card up my sleeve though, and I produced the letter given to me by my friend Mohamed in Jakarta. On reading it, the captain saluted me, said goodbye, then turned and left the hotel with his brigade of armed soldiers, taking the letter with him. I could have crumpled to the floor with relief. I'll never know what the letter said.

The following day, I caught a flight to Jayapura where, as promised, I met up with Justinius. We exchanged our contact details and he said he would stay in touch. To this day I have never since heard from him. I have tried to track him down but have not been able to find him. Later I picked up a book, *The Open Cage*, which was written about the kidnapping of a group of Westerners in Irian Jaya. Leafing through photos taken during their stay in captivity, I came across a picture of Justinius. This left me with even more questions about him than when I first met him.

CHO OYU

Tibet

Himalaya Range

8,201 metres

CHO OYU

B Y 1997 I WAS REALLY ENJOYING MY ADVENTURES. After finishing the Seven Summits, I felt restless, and I knew I needed another challenge – something to tackle that would focus my energy.

It had been nearly two years since I had climbed Mount Everest and I longed to climb another 8,000-metre mountain, again into the Death Zone, but this time without the safety net of supplementary oxygen. This had never been achieved by an Irish person, and I felt fairly confident of my ability to do it. On my trips to Everest I had been as high as 8,200 metres without oxygen, and had felt good there. That altitude was almost exactly the height of the sixth-tallest mountain in the world, Cho Oyu. 'That's it,' I remember thinking to myself.

CHO OYU

Cho Oyu is the sixth highest mountain in the world. Cho Oyu lies in the Himalayas and is 20 miles west of Mount Everest, at the border between China and Nepal. Cho Oyu means 'turquoise goddess' in Tibetan.

It was first attempted in 1952 by a legendary hero of mine, Eric Shipton, but technical difficulties at the ice cliff above 6,500 metres proved beyond the expedition's abilities. Two years later its summit was reached by Herbert Tichy, Joseph Jöchler and Sherpa Pasang Dawa Lama – all part of an Austrian expedition.

Cho Oyu from the route between Base Camp and Advance Base Camp.

I wanted a small team, with a maximum of four people. I knew that one of my climbing partners, Con Collins, also had an interest in attempting an 8,000-metre mountain. Con had climbed with me on two of my Seven Summits challenges, McKinley in Alaska and Aconcagua in South America. When asked, he jumped at the opportunity, and I was glad to have him on board. Earlier that year I had met Gavin Bate from Belfast and Eoin Sheahan from Sligo. In both of them I saw the same enthusiasm I had for climbing when I started out. Neither Con, Gavin nor Eoin had ever been on an 8,000-metre peak before, so we would be placing a huge amount of trust in each other if we were to succeed.

Twelve months later we were making our way to Nepal and into Tibet on an amazing (but dangerous) five-day bus and truck ride. Like most Himalayan trips, we travelled out of Kathmandu but this time, instead of traversing lush valleys, we climbed roads cut from the hillsides of almost solid stone. Eventually we reached the barren, desolate landscape of the Tibetan Plateau, and Base Camp at 4,800 metres.

After a few days of rest and sorting gear we loaded our yaks and headed up to Advanced Base Camp. As soon as we had a chance to acclimatise, this would be home for the duration of the expedition. Our camp overlooked the Nang Pa La pass, a vital artery that has been used for trading between Nepal and Tibet for centuries. In recent years, this pass has become an escape route for Tibetans trying to flee China's oppressive regime. While here we witnessed caravans of people being fired upon by Chinese border guards as they tried to escape, heading south into Nepal, and on to India to be close to their spiritual leader, the Dalai Lama. It was incredibly disturbing for us to see these peoples' lives threatened and be unable to do anything about it.

A few weeks into the expedition we had successfully gone higher on the mountain to Camp 1 twice, and were acknowledging how well things were going. Out of the blue, on return from one of our acclimatisation treks to stock Camp 1, a near disaster occurred. As we were returning to Base Camp a herd of yaks went wild. One of them took a dislike to Gavin for no apparent reason and hooked him with his horn under the groin. Gavin was tossed like a rag doll into the air. Luckily, it wasn't as bad as it looked. He had torn a few ligaments in his leg, but after a few days recuperating he was ready to go again and rejoin the push to stock Camp 2 with supplies. This would be our final run, and then we would be ready for our summit push.

Facing page:
Top left: Sharing a taxi in Kathmandu, from left: Gavin Bate, Con Collins and Eoin Sheehan.
Top right: Tibetan women and children.
Bottom left: Eating with some Tibetan yak herders.
Bottom right: Snowfall at Base Camp.

As we were about to leave for Camp 2 the mountain flexed its muscles. A team of Russian climbers was making an early summit attempt, and shortly into the climb one of them began to feel unwell and returned to High Camp. His teammates continued to the summit, but on their return to High Camp that evening found their other partner dead. He had suffered a burst blood vessel from being at high altitude and had bled to death. Word of this filtered down the mountain, and the story was grizzly. The burst vessel had caused blood to spray from his nose, and the inside of the tent where he lay was red. We were shocked to our boots. The trauma of this horrible incident had a psychological effect on all of us, but especially Con and Eoin.

Facing page and above: Looking towards Shishapangma from High Camp.

With heavy hearts we struck out for Camp 2, our packs gradually increasing in weight as the altitude took effect. At the base of an ice headwall, Con and Eoin decided to call it a day, retreating to Camp 1. Gavin and I progressed toward Camp 2. Midway, Gavin stopped to set up an interim camp and I continued on to cache our load at Camp 2. The following day Gavin arrived at Camp 2 intending to drop his packs and follow me back down the mountain. Gavin later decided to stay the night to acclimatise, when a storm broke. Gavin remained – trapped and stormbound – for 48 hours. Our only contact with him for those two long days was over the radio. He could not get out, and was forced to weather the storm.

That evening, another tragedy was being played out on the mountain. When the news arrived at camp, we learned that two Germans had reached the summit but, separating from each other on their way back to High Camp, only one had returned. Fears grew for the missing climber. There had already been one death on the mountain and we prayed this would not be a second. The following day it was confirmed that the missing man had died.

Any death on a mountain plays with your mind. For us, our anxiety was heightened by the fact that we were intending to summit in the Death Zone without oxygen. It's impossible to stop your mind from thinking of what might go wrong. An American climber who was ascending at the time of the German death later gave us a full recount of what happened that night. In his own words:

Prayer flags at Base Camp.

As I was going for my summit attempt, and climbing in the gully above our High Camp, I felt a belt of spindrift pouring down on me. I looked up and I could see an object falling through the air. On second glance I could see from the attire worn that it was a climber. Immediately I roared out, 'stop, stop, stop, halt, halt, halt!' I presumed it was the German. I also felt that there may have been a second person up there. The falling climber didn't make any gesture as he was tumbling and when he impacted things he didn't make any sounds or anything. And then he flew by me within 5 feet – a person's tall distance and smacked straight into the couloir and continued rolling down the hill to a stop. He didn't make a sound or anything.

Shocked again, our spirits fell as fears filled our minds. I wondered what the hell we were doing here. Why couldn't I just be happy to climb my hills at home, which I loved so much I started to doubt our resolve, our ability. In every expedition, I have come to a low point and for me this was it. I started to think of home, and my family, and the pressure it puts them under while I am away. However, being an expedition climber means you have to get over your fears and move them back into a constructive mode. Otherwise, you'll never climb anything.

After the storm, Con, Eoin and I made our way back up the mountain for our summit attempt. The weather forecast showed a window of opportunity and all camps were now stocked and secured – we were ready to go. We radioed Gavin and agreed that we would all gather at Camp 1, so Gavin descended to meet us and reunite as a team. This was it – the push was on.

The following day we moved up together, but it wasn't long before Con and Eoin started to succumb to the effects of altitude. At the base of a twenty-metre ice wall they decided to return to camp. They'd had enough of the altitude, and the effects of the two deaths played on their mind.

Gavin and I pressed on to Camp 2 again, and the following day we continued to Camp 3, entering the Death Zone. The views were spectacular, overlooking the snow-coated Himalayan chain. As we pitched our tent on 19 May we were both feeling good and knew that we had a summit push in us. This was a record for Gavin and he commented, with emotion in his voice, that he couldn't imagine that being on the summit could be any better than where we were now. We decided we would leave in the early morning hours. We ate our dinner that night in the clouds with the world at our feet. Lying in our tent with the door open, we took time to absorb the panoramic view in the sunset. Later, we prepared for our departure: crampons, ice axe, rope and rucksack were at the ready for our summit attempt.

On 20 May at 3am we left our airy tent and headed up a steep rock-strewn hillside covered with snow and ice. By 10am we were on the summit slope, with Con and Eoin watching from Base Camp through binoculars far below. Tension rose for them as we got higher and they worried for our safety. All they could do was will us up the mountain with their thoughts, and I could feel their presence. I was sad that they were not with us. We lost sight of each other as we moved onto a final, easy-angled slope. For three hours we slogged our way up, gasping for air on our way to the summit.

Then, at 1pm Gavin and I reached the pinnacle of Cho Oyu. Standing on the summit, it was amazing to see how joyous Gavin was. With tears in his eyes and hardly a voice to speak from the strenuous climb and drying effects of the thin air, all he could say was, 'We got here. We've bloody got here'. He seemed to be in disbelief. From the wide summit we could see 360-degree views of the Himalaya, and the mountains that each held such strong memories for me – Ama Dablam, where I had experienced my first major expedition, and Mera, where tragedy struck without warning; Everest, where I felt my soul had left my body for a short time. Gavin and I hugged each other in what was, for me, a magic moment on a perfect summit day.

Climber with frostbitten fingers.

115

EVEREST SOUTH SIDE

Nepal

Himalaya Range

8,850 metres

EVEREST SOUTH SIDE

A S ADVENTURES TOOK ME TO EVERY CORNER of our planet, my dream of returning to Everest never left me. For years I planned to return, and even set out the objectives I wished to fulfil if I did. But it was not until 2002 that an opportunity arose for me to go back. At the time, I was in Nepal, just preparing to return home after one of my many trekking visits to the Khumbu Valley. Ang Rita, my business partner in Nepal, turned to me and said, 'Pat, you want to climb Everest from the Nepal ' He knew bloody well that I did – we had spoken about this many times, but he had gained my attention, and he continued in his own quirky English: 'Due to a cancellation on a permit for the fiftieth anniversary of Hillary and Tenzing climb, I can get you a permit if you want it. I know it's only a few months away, what you think '

Well, that was enough to push my buttons. I asked him if he could hold it for a few weeks and I'd get back to him once I reached Ireland. I would have sixteen weeks to organise the expedition; that would be a greater challenge than climbing the mountain. I needed to get a team together – one that had the nerve to go for it, get money together to pay for it, and be committed to put their lives on hold for the next seven months. Having spoken about this for years, I knew that a number of friends would jump at the idea.

The pyramid of Everest pictured from Pumori Base Camp.

Top left: Kathmandu at dawn.
Top right: Group of local children.
Bottom left: Brightly-decorated mani stone.
Bottom right: A *sadhu* or holy man.

When I returned to Ireland in November, I rang seven friends that I thought might have the conviction to go for it. Five committed within the week. We now had a climbing team for Everest, with each person taking responsibility for an equal share in the cost of the trip. This was a test of commitment, and they all rose to the challenge, whether they begged, borrowed, stole or got sponsorship. And thus was born the Irish 2003 Everest Expedition.

The climbing team was Clare O'Leary, Hannah Shields, George Shorten, Ger McDonnell, Mick Murphy, and myself. We then got a Base Camp manager and assistant – Pat Duggan and John Joyce. My office, under the leadership of Niall Foley and Gill Roche, would look after PR and communications. I pulled every contact I knew from my fellow adventurers around the world to get the gear we required. We ordered tents from America, specialised food from England, oxygen from Russia, and so much more. All the climbers guaranteed the money personally, so we announced our plans through a press release. Then a sponsorship committee was put in place under the direction of two other friends – Dave Twomey and Pat Fenton. We all worked day and night, and in what seemed like the blink of an eye we departed Cork airport in a blaze of publicity.

This time we tackled Everest from the south side, via the South-Southeast Ridge, coming from Nepal. Our team had three objectives:

1. To have the first Irish woman summit Mount Everest

2. To be the first Irish team to succeed from Nepal

3. To be the first Irishman to reach the summit from both sides: Tibet and Nepal

The expedition succeeded in re-living Hillary and Tenzing's heroic 1953 pioneering journey to the top of the world. We ascended from Base Camp, through the Western Cwm to the South Col, up the Hillary Step onto the summit. This was an amazing triumph, made all the better because we had put the expedition together in only sixteen weeks.

In what I consider an enormous success, four of my team reached the summit: Mick Murphy from Cork, Ger McDonnell from Limerick and two of my Sherpa friends Pemba Gyalji and Pemba Rinzee.

Without a doubt the most important members of our expedition were our teammates from Nepal. All were personal friends of mine that I had climbed and worked with on trips to Nepal. Their loyalty and expertise at high altitude is incredible. Pemba Gyalji was in charge of the Sherpa team and held joint responsibility with me for logistics on the mountain. They were an integral part of the expedition, and without their participation and hard work it would have been impossible for us to succeed. We were delighted with the success but we were also disappointed that we all didn't reach the summit.

Hannah Shields, a dentist from Derry, climbed successfully to 27,500 feet but was forced to descend due to frostbite. She would later successfully summit Everest on 19 May 2007.

Team member George Shorten from Cork developed acute mountain sickness at 24,000 feet and, sadly, had to be evacuated.

The Irish team on the Hillary Step at 28,750 feet in 2004 from where Pat Falvey had retreated in 2003.

Clare O'Leary ascended on her final summit attempt to 24,000 feet and, ironically (as a gastroenterologist) had to descend due to a stomach bug.

My own summit attempt that year was no better. Upon reaching the bottom of Hillary Step at 28,770 feet, I had to turn — just one hour from the summit. Due to problems with my oxygen flow, I developed pulmonary oedema and cerebral oedema. Eventually I became hypoxic, and lost my peripheral vision, completely unable to distinguish where to place my feet. I was like a drunk on top of the world. In a comatose condition, I had to make one of the hardest decisions of my life, and that was to descend. So close and yet so far, experience had taught me never be greedy. I was also aware that this is where another friend, Rob Hall, had perished in 1996 while speaking by radio to his wife about the name they should call their daughter. He pushed it just a little too far. Alarm bells were ringing in my head; descend, descend ... the expedition is a success.

For me this was one of the proudest days of my life as I watched my teammates cross the Hillary Step – the last obstacle they would face summit bound. I imagined every step they were taking, and every emotion they would be feeling.

Descending, I sobbed with emotion, knowing I was right on the brink of dying, and hoping I hadn't left it too late. I was never so scared as I turned for home, stumbling and at times crawling along the narrow ridge on top of the world. Clinging to the rope that had been fixed down the Southeast Ridge, this thin life line kept me on track. I was as good as blind in this condition. Luckily, I had a skilled team behind me and I knew if

I could stay focused help would soon be there. Later, on their descent from the summit, Ger McDonell and the two Pembas assisted me back to the South Col. If it wasn't for their help I'm sure I would not have made it back to High Camp that day. I will be forever indebted to them for their skill and patience in looking after me that near-fatal evening.

The Khumbu Ice Fall with Mick Murphy and Clare O'Leary near one of its leaning towers of ice.

Everest Base Camp at 17,500 feet, with the Khumbu Glacier behind.

By the time I returned to Base Camp I had made a full recovery. As expedition leader I felt satisfied and happy with the result of our expedition. We had much to be proud of, having met an important historical objective by being the first Irish team to summit on the South side of Everest. I thanked the gods of the mountain for another safe journey, and for granting us all a safe passage down.

However, just on our return to Base Camp, Clare approached me and expressed a desire to return. She felt she could summit if given another chance and asked me if I would lead another attempt on Everest. Turning back so close to the peak had left her with a craving to reach the summit, and I recognised this type of yearning from my own first attempt at Everest. Reflecting on what had gone wrong, I knew I, too, could summit again if I had the chance. And we still had two objectives to complete, I thought to myself. Never a person to give up easily, I immediately took up the challenge, and thus was born the Irish WYETH Everest Expedition 2004.

IRISH WYETH EVEREST EXPEDITION 2004

Early in the year logistics and planning began. Another permit was granted, and the whole process began again. Oxygen had to be ordered from Russia, food from England, and tents from America. Our new website was launched, communication systems were put in place, and a press and sponsorship drive was initiated. Thankfully, Wyeth sponsored the expedition. The other members of my previous team were far too busy to return, and this time I wanted a smaller team of only three climbers: Clare, John Joyce – who had served as Base Camp manager for the 2003 Everest Expedition – and me. This year Adrian Rahill from Ennis served as Base Camp manager and Sheila Kavanagh from Galway as assistant. Niall Foley was again on technical support.

We left Ireland on 17 March. It was an emotional departure. This time our parents were all more aware of the dangers of Everest. Clare's father Kevin O'Leary wished us the best, and with tears in his eyes, asked me to please ensure his daughter came back safely. The pressures on those at home were nearly as great as for those on the mountain.

The remains of the helicopter which crashed, injuring eight and killing one, on the Khumbu Glacier. We had flown in the helicopter just hours before.

The mess tent in 2004 doubled as a communications HQ, from left: Sheila Cavanagh, Tim Orr and Clare O'Leary.

Looking down on Namche Bazaar, the commercial village between Nepal and Tibet and eleven days' walk from the nearest road head.

KHUMBU VALLEY TREK

From Kathmandu, we flew over the lower foothills of the Himalaya to Lukla, the starting point for our trek.

We landed at Lukla on an airstrip built on the side of a cliff face, adjoining this small Himalayan village (an exciting adventure in itself!). We began the process of unpacking our equipment, checked and double checked all our provisions and gear, hired 70 yaks and 50 porters, and started our journey to Base Camp.

Leaving Lukla, we embarked on an eleven-day trek, meandering through the foothills of the upper Khumbu. We walked along the banks of the famous rivers of the Dudh Kosi and Bhote Kosi, surrounded by imposing gorges. Torrential rivers rushed through them as we made our way to the Everest region. During our journey, we stayed in villages and lived amongst the indigenous people of the area. Each day's trek was more spectacular than the day before. Mountains projected like massive pillars from the deep valleys, and we made our way along narrow paths etched from the steep hillsides.

We were trekking in an area steeped in mountaineering history. In the distance, at the top of the valley, Mount Everest beckoned, protected by the mighty Nuptse-Lhotse Ridge. I turned my head and saw Thamserku – the mountain of the ten summits, Kangtega – saddle mountain, and Ama Dablam – mother's charm.

This is the heart of the most beautiful and inspiring mountain range in the world, the Himalayas: 'home of the snows'. They stretch in a great arch across Asia, 150 miles wide and 1,700 miles long, from the Indus in the west to the Brahmaputra in the east. All along the length of the Himalaya, the mountaintops are revered as a place of the gods by the people of the valleys below. We were travelling in an area that for centuries has been the setting for epic feats of exploration and mountain climbing.

After arriving at Base Camp we unpacked all our gear, checking and re-checking each item to ensure we had all provisions in place. Every item had to be accounted for to survive in this hostile environment for 65 days. We said farewell to our trekking support team here, and then the real work of climbing the mountain began.

We established Base Camp at the barren and rocky base of the Khumbu Ice Fall. This would be our new home away from home; a place that we would leave and return to many times as we made the switchback climb to the various camps up the mountain. This back-breaking approach of climbing high and sleeping low had a two-fold purpose: it enabled us to acclimatise to high altitude, and while doing so we stocked the camps with supplies for the journey to the top of Everest and back. Therefore, we couldn't just climb Mount Everest once, but had to make many trips up and down the mountain to finally get to High Camp – and a shot at the summit.

This year we made fourteen trips through the Khumbu Ice Fall, which is the scariest, and yet most beautiful place on the mountain. A spectacular but treacherous horror-chamber of bottomless crevasses, seracs and ice blocks, it goes from 18,000 feet to 21,000 feet. Chunks of ice as large as houses lie among free-standing ice walls up to 30 feet high, and are negotiated with the aid of fixed ropes and aluminium ladders. The ice-fall is an ever-changing maze, and on more then one occasion we experienced scary moments as we edged our way to Camp 1.

Left: Looking up the Lhotse Face from near Camp 2.
Camp 3 can be seen in the centre.

Top: The Western Cwm with Lhotse in the background

Above: The view down from Camp 3 on the Lhotse Face to the Western Cwm and Pumori.

CAMP 1

The ice-fall leads to Camp 1 – *The Silent Valley*, also known as the Western Cwm. This vast, flat area of endless snow is a massive glacial snowfield of deep crevasses and mountain walls, frequently washed by avalanches. The sun here reflects off the walls of Nuptse and the western buttress of Everest, paradoxically generating powerful heat, despite the freezing ambient temperatures. Nightfall brings deep, murmuring, cracking sounds beneath the tents as crevasses open and close deep down in the glacier below.

CAMP 2

Camp 2 is a bleak, desolate spot marked by a rocky patch at the foot of the icy Lhotse wall, at the upper end of the Western Cwm. This place is absolutely stunning in good weather but most unwelcoming in bad. Clouds roll in from the lower ranges of the Himalaya, up the valley and gather here. At times, the winds here can be violent enough to destroy tents, or even whole camps.

CAMP 3

Camp 3 is at Lhotse wall, a 4,000-foot high wall of sheer blue ice, which is climbed using fixed ropes. Early in the season, prior to acclimatisation, this wall can be a major ordeal. It leads to Camp 3, a narrow platform placed right out of the wall. A traverse then leads to a distinctively coloured rocky section known as the Yellow Band – the world's highest fault – just before the Geneva Spur and Camp 4.

CAMP 4

At 26,000 feet, Camp 4, in the South Col, is frequently besieged by ferocious winds. Reaching here means you are close to the final part of the climb.

John Joyce descending to Base Camp through Khumbu Ice Fall.

SUMMIT DAY

It was 17 May 2004. We arrived at High Camp at 1pm after many days of pushing ourselves to the limit. Clare was delighted to have passed her high point from the previous year, and I was apprehensive about being back in Death Zone at the South Col. All our focus was on the weather, and Adrian at Base Camp was in constant telephone contact with Michael Fagin in Seattle, one of the best forecasters in the world on mountain weather. We were told the jet stream wind should hold off for 24 hours, then descend on the mountain again. This meant we had a 24-hour window to reach the summit and get back down to Base Camp. That advice was good enough for me. All we had to do now was sit and wait until evening and make the final decision.

Clare and I sat, uncomfortably, as we twisted and turned in our tent, not saying much to each other and in deep contemplation of what the night might hold in store. We pondered our own fears, and our ability to reach the summit. The pressure was immense, with many people following our progress in the press and on the Internet. Irish people watched in particular for Clare; if she reached the summit, she would be the first Irish female to do so.

Our satellite phone was busy as we relayed our position, and Clare had just received a phone call with a message from our president, Mary McAleese, sending her best wishes on our summit attempt and reminding us to go safely. We spoke to our families and knew that they would not sleep until we were back.

I watched Clare boiling water so that we could re-hydrate, and I wondered what was going through her mind. I have never climbed with a person as focused and committed, and I couldn't believe that tonight my climbing partner, of only 5 foot 3 inches and only weighing 53 kg, was going for the summit.

Soon we both needed rest, and my mind drifted in and out of a hazy dream world. I pondered what brought us to this crazy place, where our bodies were suffering from oxygen starvation. Gasping for air and trying to concentrate on the final stages of the climb, I went through each step of the moves I made the year before, and I guided Clare through a visualisation of the climb ahead, to lesson the tension. I knew we would have many more hours of punishing, snail-paced work ahead of us if we were going to succeed.

We rested, waiting to make the final decision to go or retreat from the mountain. Thoughts flooded my mind of the friends I had lost on this mountain. I questioned the rationale behind my own desire to risk our lives for twenty minutes or so of personal glory on top of the world.

Clare O'Leary on oxygen at the South Col.

It was just the two of us now in the tent, because our third climbing partner, John Joyce, had developed acute mountain sickness at Camp 1 and had to descend.

I began to think about Rob Hall, Scott Fisher, and Michael Reinberger, who lay in icy graves in the Death Zone above us. I thought about how Clare's father had asked me to ensure nothing would happen to his daughter. If Clare succeeded, she would enter the history books as the first Irish woman to summit Everest. The whole country was behind her, but no one would think less of her if she returned to Base Camp. The mental pressure on her was enormous as she, too, struggled with the decision of whether or not to go for it. Tension was high.

I knew the negative thoughts needed to be erased from my mind if I was to be prepared for the summit. I began to focus on more constructive thoughts. I knew that we were capable of climbing this mountain. I had been above this height three times before. I knew how my body was feeling, and I was ready. I had worked with Clare, and I knew how she was feeling and that she was also ready. I made the decision that, from here on in, if we were to leave this campsite the summit would not be the goal, but instead our goal would be to return safely to Base Camp. If at any point I was unsure of Clare's ability or my own, I would turn, remembering how close I was to death the previous time.

My Sherpa team had also arrived at the South Col that evening, and were camped not far from were we were. At 8pm I got a radio call from Pemba. 'Come in Pat, come in Clare, what are your plans. We are going for it and will leave in an hour.' With that news, it seemed so simple all of a sudden: the summit push was about to begin.

At 9pm we exited into the pitch-black abyss of night. After being cocooned in our tent, the exposure to the bitter cold shocked our bodies. The oxygen from our breath was freezing on our masks, and the only way to allow a flow was to break off the icicles that formed. I was delighted that four of my Sherpa team had also decided to go for the summit.

With fingers and toes freezing, we continued summit-bound on a night that seemed to last forever. There was only one other team on the mountain that night – an American guide with a client and two Sherpas. We passed them not far from the South Col moving slowly. At 1am we arrived ahead of schedule to an area named The Balcony, which is the start of the crest of the South -east Ridge. Later in the day an American-Bolivian climber from the other team would die here on his return. An incoming storm, exhaustion and bad decisions were to cost him his life.

Just below us on the ridge we passed the body of my friend Scott Fisher. Through exhaustion, Scott had died on his return from the summit in 1996. He now lay preserved in ice for eternity. This was a stark reminder that reaching the summit is only the halfway point of the journey.

Sherpas Pemba Gyalji, Lama Babu, Jangbu, Lhakpa and Nang Chumbi.

At 6.45am on 18 May, Clare O'Leary became the first Irish woman to reach the highest point on Earth while Pat became one of a handful of adventurers to summit from both the Nepalese and Tibetan sides.

Below: Pat Falvey pucked a sliothar from the summit down the icy slopes of Mount Everest.

We were now on the narrow Southeast Ridge – the most dangerous section of the climb – with thousands of feet of fall on both sides. Our confidence was growing as twilight turned to sunrise, and below us the mountain range opened up to a sight of grandeur, revealing ice-capped mountaintops protruding through puffed clouds as we crossed the spectacular upper reaches of the mountain. Approaching the South Summit, we descended about 30 feet to cross a sweeping traverse leading to the main crux of the ridge – the Hillary Step. All the team were going well and I knew we had it in the bag. It was amazing climbing over this section – it had been etched in my mind since I first began to think of climbing this mountain. It was so spectacular to actually make the famous move, at nearly 29,000 feet. I was in my element and enjoying every minute of the climb. Once we were over the crux, I was overcome with emotion as I had passed my high point of 2003, and the place I thought I'd die. I put my head in my hand and cried as the memories of last year came flooding back.

Realising this was not a place to linger, I pulled myself together and started moving again. I could see Clare ahead and for another 45 minutes we slogged upward until eventually I could only see the sky. I waited for a moment just below the summit and once again said

a prayer for all of those who had reached the summit and hadn't returned. Then, taking a few deep breaths, and with a final last surge, I gained the top of the world. I looked at my watch and it was 6.45am. I was surprised that we had made such a speedy ascent.

Clare, Jangbu Sherpa, Lama Babu Sherpa, Pemba Gyalji Sherpa, and Nang Chumbi Sherpa and I stood on top of the world. We hugged and took photos. As I put my camera away, I took from my rucksack a hurley and a sliotar. Even though I was exhausted and feared I'd miss it, I connected beautifully and belted the ball from the highest point on earth, into the rarefied atmosphere and down the icy slopes of Mount Everest. This became part of Irish history as the world's highest *puc fada*, breaking my teammate's record of 2003, when Ger McDonnell hit the sliotar from the South Col at 26,000 feet.

We then sat on the summit for a small while and rested, not wanting to leave. I reached my hand into my breast pocket and took from it my Irish Tricolour. Tying it to my ice axe, I clenched it in my fist and held it high with pride and waved it in the air. We had really done it. We had achieved our goal, and I was shaking with excitement as I hugged Clare. We were the highest people on earth. I was so proud, not just for myself, but for my Sherpa team who had worked so hard right throughout the expedition, and had gained an audience with their goddess. For Clare, who had dreamed and dreamed big, she was now the first Irish woman to reach the top of the highest mountain in the world.

At this stage, a storm was brewing and we were caught in the eye as clouds curled just above our heads. The jet stream winds were returning and it was time to descend. We had made our dream a reality – we had succeeded and now it was time to go home.

Reaching the summit of Everest was an amazing experience for me. In 2003 I was forced to turn back at 24,000 feet. on because of illness. When I returned in 2004, I was even more determined and focused on giving the mountain my best shot. I felt more relaxed, and was able to really enjoy the climb.

There were many tough days, but the final days of the summit bid went well. I have very clear and spectacular memories of the Summit Ridge and reaching the summit itself. It's a moment I will never forget – overwhelming emotion and excitement – and safely sharing the summit as a team was the perfect prize for such an extreme test of endurance.

We had no idea how much interest there was in the expedition back home, being to a large extent isolated from the media while on the mountain. On returning to Ireland, I couldn't believe the support, interest and enthusiasm of the huge numbers of people who had followed our journey. It was hard to believe all the letters, cards, emails and visits from well-wishers. It was great to experience first-hand the loyalty and positive energy that our nation can generate. Thank you to all our supporters.

CLARE O'LEARY

Pumori
7145m

Shishapangma
8016m

Cho Oyu
8153m

Gyachung Kang
7922m

Rongbuk Glacier

Chomo-Lonzo
7780m

Makalu
8462m

Lhotse
8516m

Changtse
7580m

East Rongbuk Glacier

N. E. Ridge

Chamlang
7319m

S. E. Ridge

Ama Dablam
6812m

Thamserku
6623m

Nuptse
7849m

On 18 May 2004 I took my camera and pivoted on the highest point on earth, north, south, east and west. I was elated and in awe of my surroundings as I took these shots of the greatest mountain range in the world. I was so proud as an Irishman and a Corkman to be, for a short time, on the highest point on Earth.

MOUNT VINSON

South Georgia, Antarctica

Sentinel Range

4,892 metres

Mount Vinson, the highest peak in the Antarctic.

WE HAD BEEN ISSUED WITH A 48-hour storm warning while on the mountain, and we knew we had a very short window of time to reach the safety of Base Camp. If we made it, we could catch a small aircraft back to Patriot Hills Base Camp, where a Hercules aircraft would await us. If we didn't make it, it would mean weathering an Antarctic storm without even the basic amenities of Base Camp. This was life or death.

Exposed as we were in the middle of this icy continent, we stood little chance of surviving. We would have to push hard to make it to Base Camp. The problem was that we were already exhausted, having just reached the summit of Mount Vinson that day.

My climbing partners on Vinson were Jean Luc Neidergang, Thierry Reinard, Jeff Shea and Michael Jerjensen. We advanced slowly through the night, against high winds and over rough, icy ground to finally arrive in Base Camp the following day. We were all totally exhausted, freezing cold and in a state of serious

MOUNT VINSON

Vinson Massif is the highest mountain of Antarctica, located about 1,200km (750 miles) from the South Pole. The mountain is about 21km (13 miles) long and 13km (8 miles) wide. The southern end of the massif is capped by Mount Craddock (4,650m).

It is in the Sentinel Range of the Ellsworth Mountains, which stand above the Ronne Ice Shelf near the base of the Antarctic Peninsula.

The massif's existence was unsuspected until 1957, when it was spotted by US Navy aircraft. It was named after Carl Vinson (also the namesake of an aircraft carrier), a United States Georgia Congressman who was a key supporter of funding for Antarctic research.

dehydration. It took every bit of resolve and concentration we had to put together our tent. When we finally managed, we fell into it in the falling light of the evening. As soon as the sun dipped below the horizon, temperatures plummeted from –15 to –40 degrees Celsius. Even though we were back in our tent, our bodies didn't have enough energy left to re-heat ourselves. I remember thinking it was a mistake not to warm up before sleeping, but exhaustion had rendered us incapable of doing anything else.

Patriot Hills, main starting point for Vinson expedition.

Top left: Pat Falvey (left) with colleagues at Patriot Hills.

Top right: Mount Elias range showing a peak above ice cap.

Left: Pat Falvey during his first Antarctic trip.

Right: Pat Falvey on Vinson Summit, 1997.

Mount Vinson Base Camp, with Vinson summit centre background.

Lying in my tent, I felt colder than I had ever been before in my life. My body shook and shivered uncontrollably, and every now and then I would go into a sudden violent spasm of jerking.

Afraid and fearful of what the night had in store, I prayed that I would make it through the night. I knew that all my energy would have to be focused on surviving in my hypothermic state. I had seen other climbers in the same condition, and I knew what to do — I needed to stay positive, not give up hope of survival, and conserve energy. I lay in the foetal position, focusing on my hands, which were in front of my face. My eyelids were freezing up, but I fell into a trance-like state, remaining focused on my gloves through the haze of ice.

Slowly, the sun came up, warming my tent and seeping warmth into my body. I began to feel the blood moving back into my extremities. And just like those I have seen suffering from acute mountain sickness, before I knew it, I was not only feeling better – but I was fine!

Oddly, the whole time in the tent, I could have called for help at any moment. I was in Base Camp! I have seen this sort of thing happen many times on expedition; people dying when help was right next to them. Your energy becomes so focused on surviving that you bypass logic completely.

Top: Adventurers and their gear packed into the Russian aircraft.

Middle: From left, Pat Falvey, Clare O'Leary and John Dowd with the Russian Ilyushin at Patriot Hills in the Antarctic, 2006.

Bottom: Bad weather at Patriot Hills.

Once drawn to Antarctica, you'll always want to go back. It is, without question, the most spectacular, loneliest and most remote region on earth. There is nowhere else like it. It's so beautiful – but when the Antarctic turns on you, it can quickly become hell.

On my flight home from this adventure, I sat beside an American woman named Nancy. Although I was speaking to her for a while, it took me a long time to notice she was somewhat elderly. Eventually I asked her age.

'Seventy-three,' she smiled. Naturally, I wondered what she was doing on the plane.

'I've been fascinated by Arctic and Antarctic explorers ever since I was a young girl,' she replied, 'and I wanted to see what it was like to stand on the North Pole and the South Pole before I died.' In August she took a ship to the North Pole, and now, because 'us adventurers' had chartered flights to Antarctica, she was able to fly right to the South Pole. 'We landed, I got out, and now I have been to the South Pole.'

Amazing. Seventy-three years of age and she'd been to both poles. I wondered how she could afford this and she happily explained that her husband died when she was 65. She promised herself then that she would see her dreams through while she still could. So, she sold her home to pay for the expeditions! When I asked what she was going to do for money in the future, she replied that she had raised six children, and that she hoped they would keep her 'in the style in which I raised them.' What a woman!

In December 2006, I was lucky enough to be on my way to Antarctica once again. This time, it would be as expedition leader on Clare O'Leary's Seven Summits Challenge. We brought a small team; John Dowd, who we climbed with on Mount McKinley, Clare and myself.

A thrilling flight brought us to the interior of Antarctica. A hodgepodge of adventurers packed into a Russian Ilyushin aircraft – Russians, Norwegians, French, Koreans and, of course, the Irish team. Some were walking to the South Pole, some skiing the last degrees of longitude and latitude on earth. Others just came to visit Patriot Hills and others, like us, to climb Mount Vinson. On our no-frills flight, we sat on seats along the outer edges of the plane like paratroopers going to war. Oxygen masks were stuck behind the seats in case of emergency, and life jackets were on our laps, constantly ready.

All our gear had to be stored in the centre of the plane to balance the weight on this massive sixteen-wheeled giant. With eight hours ahead of us on the most dangerous flight on earth, we left South America en route to our ice runway at Patriot Hills, just 200 miles from Mount Vinson. This flight is one of the most expensive on earth. But the flight and the scenery were magnificent. We took turns going to the cockpit to relieve boredom, and look out the window. Blue seas turned to thousands of small icebergs, and finally we flew over solid pack ice.

The landing is the most dangerous part of the flight; there are no paved runways but only flat, solid ice. We got excited as our pilot announced our descent and we all held on tightly as we prepared to land. We felt a massive thud upon impact, and then a bumpy ride on corrugated ice for the next few minutes. The plane eventually came to a gravity stop – unable to use brakes – because doing so could cause the plane to flip or go out of control.

A few days later we were out in the snowy wonderland, working our way from Base Camp to Camp 1 on the Vinson Massif. After establishing camp, we left some provisions here in the event of emergency: spare tent, stove and some food.

Arriving at Camp 1, we could leave nothing to chance in the unpredictable weather conditions of this continent. We set up our tent, and built thick snow walls around it for protection against extreme winds. After a peaceful night, our intention was to carry a load to the bottom of the ice wall at Camp 2 and return to Camp 1 for the rest of the day.

The following morning, there were ominous signs of bad weather, and the winds increased, cancelling our plan. The ferocity of the winds grew during the day to a full-blown storm, with the infamous katabatic winds reaching well beyond gale force.

Protected in our cocoon, Clare, John and I tried to pass the time playing cards. This was a great way to ease the tension of being stuck in the tent. Luckily, we had reinforced the protection around our tent with 5-foot high walls made of 3-foot thick snow blocks. We were confident we had done enough to withstand the winds, which howled down on us.

There is nothing like sitting in a tent during the height of a storm and wondering if your little home will weather it. Experience had taught me never to relax in storms – to always be on alert. At the very moment we were discussing how strong our tent was, and how many storms it had survived in winds of over 100 miles an hour, a sudden shift in wind direction and an increase in ferocity changed everything. Out of the blue, a massive gust lifted a 3-foot snow block, hurtling it through the air and onto our tent. In panic, I roared out to grab the poles to steady the tension on them.

We reached out and put our hands against the outer sheet of the tent to ease the pressure on the poles and stop them from breaking. Then a second block hit our tent right on one of the poles. It cracked in two. This was serious — the structure of our tent was damaged and we needed to work fast to repair it.

We rapidly pulled on our protective down gear, to get out into the storm to fix the damaged tent. John and I forced our way into the cold while Clare braced the poles from the inside. Then another snow block hit the tent, cracking a second pole. We were trying our best to repair the tears and broken poles with duct tape and to strengthen the snow walls again. The wind was horrific and the blizzard conditions were blurring our vision, so that even through protective goggles we struggled.

Just when we managed to recover, I heard another loud crack – two more poles snapped, shooting straight through the outer layer of the tent and ripping the fly sheet in four places. We were in deep trouble. The tent was beyond repair at this point, our protection destroyed. Our only hope was to collapse the tent and use it as a bivouac shelter. John and I found the zipper to the inside of the tent and crawled under it, exhausted and battered from the storm.

Inside, we put all our clothes on, climbed into our sleeping bags and pushed together like spoons to try to keep warm. The winds howled on for another 24 hours. Every two hours we had to exit our improvised bivy shelter to dig away the spindrift that was burying our tent.

We knew we had no choice but to retreat. Our stove had frozen, our tent was a write-off, and we were dehydrated and completely exhausted. Salvaging what we could and burying stocks that we didn't need immediately, we descended to Base Camp to retrieve our spare tent, gas stove and supplies.

After two days of rest the weather eased, and we moved back up the mountain in fabulous conditions. We made it to Camp 1 again, rested and continued on to Camp 2, where we left our sleds behind. From there, we hiked up an impressive but easy snow slope to Camp 3. The view was breathtaking as we looked at the Ronne Ice Shelf, Mount Shin and Mount Vinson. We rested here for the day to acclimatise before we attempted the summit.

Top: Clare O'Leary and John Dowd.
Middle: Camp 1 with the tent wrecked by the storm.
Bottom: Sled hauling.

Clare O'Leary and John Dowd departing the summit with Jaca Peak in the background.

John Dowd, Clare O'Leary and Pat Falvey on Vinson Summit.

From here our climb to the summit took us over a gently sloping glacier, and up a moderate climb to the Summit Ridge. We trudged along the narrow line of this ridge and reached the summit at last, taking in the views the whole way up. Clare, John and I hugged and congratulated each other when we reached the summit.

This was the final leg of Clare's challenge to reach the highest summits on each of seven continents. She became the first Irish female to do so and the fifteenth woman ever. This also completed my second time of climbing the Seven Summits. Later, I discovered I was to be only the fourth person in the world to have achieved this.

Mount Vinson in Antarctica was my final peak of the Seven Summits. It was my first time visiting this continent, and I have never seen anywhere so vast and yet so uniquely beautiful. Our final expedition wasn't easy – we were hit by high winds and lost a tent – but once the weather improved, things went in our favour once again. It was hard to believe, as I stood on the summit of Vinson, that the Seven Summits Challenge was over. I didn't want it to be in lots of ways!

I'd had an amazing time travelling the world and climbing some beautiful mountains with great friends and, of course, with Pat as expedition leader. But now it was time for a new adventure!

CLARE O'LEARY

BEYOND ENDURANCE

Antarctica

BEYOND ENDURANCE

THE IDEA WAS TO TAKE ORDINARY men and women – not people with expedition, climbing, or even hillwalking experience – just ordinary people, and see if they could complete an expedition to Antarctica. Two years of planning went into the Beyond Endurance Expedition, and we really had no idea if anyone would be interested. There were certainly some catches: although no experience was required, members would have to learn the necessary skills. They also had to pay their own way through the training, with no guarantees that they would be picked. Would anyone be willing to participate. There was nothing left to do but place ads and hope for the best.

The advertisement seeking volunteers, which appeared in newspapers and outdoor magazines.

Left: The Beyond Endurance team trekking on Ronge Island, Antarctica.

IN THE FOOTSTEPS OF OUR HEROES

The Beyond Endurance Expedition was influenced by my love of Antarctica and the unsung Irish polar explorers: Tom Crean, Robert Ford, Patrick Keohane, Tim and Mortimer McCarthy and, in particular, Ernest Shackleton – one of my all-time favourite heroes as a leader of men. It was to be a tribute to the many Irish Antarctic heroes, as well as the pioneering leaders from all around the world with whom they served. Our men played a significant role in exploring the Antarctic continent, forever immortalising our presence there with Irish names dotting the charts and the surrounding seas.

The route we would follow was steeped in history, retracing some of the most dramatic events to take place at the beginning of Antarctic exploration. In 1915, Ernest Shackleton set out from Buenos Aires with the intent of sailing to the island of South Georgia, and from there through the Weddell Sea to Vahsel Bay, where they hoped to cross roughly 1,800 miles of Antarctica by foot — traversing the entire continent over the South Pole — to reach the Ross Sea.

Unfortunately, savage weather conditions trapped their boat in thick ice. Drifting with the ice flow for nine months, their boat was finally crushed, sinking in November 1915. Left with only a lifeboat, the crew finally reached shore at South Georgia, starving and needing urgent help. Shackleton, Tom Crean and Frank Worsley were forced to traverse the icy island to seek rescue. The first objective of our expedition was to follow their path — to retrace Shackleton's courageous journey by traversing South Georgia.

I also wanted to complete Shackleton's dream: in 1907-1909 Shackleton intended to traverse the entire continent, passing over the South Pole. He reached as far as the polar plateau, 97 miles short of the South Pole, before having to turn back. I would pick one of the Beyond Endurance team members to journey with Clare O'Leary and myself to complete his expedition to the South Pole and beyond. We would ski, snowshoe, climb and kite from the Weddell Sea to the South Pole – and beyond – passing Shackleton's southernmost point.

WHEN THE WAITING WAS OVER ...

I was amazed at the scale of interest when we finally launched the expedition — 2,500 applications were submitted. Now we had an even greater problem on our hands than if we had too few applications. Over 750 applicants sought the South Georgia traverse, and the rest were for the support crew.

ORDINARY PEOPLE ACHIEVING EXTRAORDINARY THINGS

Applicants wishing to traverse South Georgia had to commit to serious physical and mental training. Over a period of fourteen months, a series of trials based in Ireland and Norway were held to assess and determine who would make the final team.

Eventually, we were able to narrow the prospective adventurers for the traverse down to 25, which were those who had trained and passed all the assessments on skills required. The support team was picked on a first-come basis, made up of enthusiastic men, women and even children.

An iceberg viewed from the deck of MV *Ushuaia*.

At the grave of Ernest Shackleton in South Georgia.

Just as we were about to leave we got another surprise: RTÉ, the Irish national television network, commissioned a mini series on the progress of these adventurers. It would cover the training and follow their journey to Antarctica

SETTING SAIL – HISTORY IN THE MAKING

The expedition now had 80 team members — the largest Irish Antarctic expedition ever — and we set out on 6 November 2006. The eldest member of our party, Fergus, was in his mid seventies and the youngest, Eve, was just eight years of age.

Arriving at the southern tip of South America, we boarded our ship, the *Ushuaia*. The excitement was electrifying – and with a final blow from the ship's horn the journey to Antarctica began. Our course was taking us to the last great wilderness, isolated by ice, wind and the wild seas of the Southern Ocean. All were out on deck for our journey through the scenic Beagle Channel, heading east towards the Drake Passage.

For three days we followed Shackleton's original route to South Georgia, wowed by the wildlife that surrounded us. Wandering, black-browed, and sooty albatrosses, shearwaters, giant and cape petrels and numerous other seabirds accompanied us towards the Antarctic Convergence, the biological barrier where cold polar waters sink beneath the warmer waters of the temperate zones.

The Beyond Endurance team gearing up for the traverse of South Georgia.

SOUTH GEORGIA

This island boasts much of the geographical and biological diversity of Antarctica, including awe-inspiring scenery, with towering, 7,000-foot mountains and mighty glaciers. The island attracts an astounding concentration of wildlife and is considered by many to be one of the most interesting wildlife sanctuaries on earth. Our approach to the east coast was heralded by thousands of king penguins, with rugged snow-covered mountains providing a dramatic backdrop for this marvellous scene.

THE PLAN – TEAMS SPLIT

While the crossing party attempted to cross South Georgia, the support crew remaining onboard would make Zodiac landings on King Haakon Bay. They would then attempt other landings in the Salisbury Plain, and Gold Harbour, where huge numbers of king penguins and elephant seals gather to breed, also visiting Prion Island to view nesting wandering albatross. Finally, at Fortuna Bay, the entire team would reunite and march across the last section of the traverse together. Our journey to pay homage to our heroes would end at Stromness, where Shackleton lies buried.

THE TRAVERSE OF SOUTH GEORGIA – DAY 1

A wake up call at 4.30am roused us from our bunks. We dressed, then filed to the bridge. In the dead of night our captain had carefully navigated us into King Haakon Bay, and we were all keen to catch the first glimpse of South Georgia. It was a bitterly cold morning with winds of 40-50 knots per hour, but people were buzzing with excitement.

As South Georgia came into view, we gaped in awe. Words that came to mind were cold, inhospitable and unwelcoming. Snow-capped mountains stretched down to the sea, with the amazing colours of sunrise softening the vistas.

The weather looked ominous. We had three official forecasts, none of which looked good:

Day 1:   30-40 knots per hour from the northwest; cloud base at 500 metres.

Day 2:   25-30 knots, easing to the southwest.

Day 3:   35-45 knots, from the southwest.

Day 4-6: Worsening until the end of the week.

We also couldn't predict what effect these local conditions would have further into our journey, and how the katabatic (downward) winds might impede our traverse.

Although it was our first time seeing penguins and seals, we didn't really have time to appreciate them. We needed to make the most of every working hour from here on out.

Making our way up the sloping shore, conditions changed dramatically – the wind disappeared, and we enjoyed clear blue skies.

Moving north of the Shackleton Gap we reached snow. Putting on our snowshoes, we roped up in teams of five to six people. We moved together and kept up a good speed; although weather conditions were fine, we knew well how fleeting this could be.

Crossing the Crean Glacier in high winds.

About four hours later, as we crossed the Murray Snowfield, we saw dark, threatening clouds forming to our left, making their way up the valley. The winds began to gust.

At 4.30 we were approaching the Trident Ridge; we could see the three towers ahead of us as we headed up the long, steep slope to the top of the ridge. This is where Crean, Shackleton and Worsley were forced to slide down on their rope without knowing what was below them. At this stage, the cloud had really come in. Visibility was down to 15-20 metres and winds were gusting 40-50kmph. It was particularly difficult to drag sleds over the top section and everyone struggled. Finally reaching the far side of the ridge, we paused and removed our snowshoes for the descent.

By the time we got to the bottom, it was snowing – a really wet snow that soaked everything through – and the winds picked up to 60-70kmph. All gear had to be firmly anchored.

We set up camp as quickly as we could. Before long, there were shouts of panic as tent poles snapped, but some quick repairs kept us safe for the moment. We were wet, cold and tired, but at least well fed and sheltered.

THE TRAVERSE OF SOUTH GEORGIA – DAY 2

The following morning we were on the move at 5am. We had suffered a long cold, windy, wet night. Broken poles had torn some of our tents during the night, and no amount of duct tape would repair them. The weather and wind had still not improved, and conditions were trying as we attempted to minimise any further losses.

It was about 8.30am before we were ready to leave. As we put on our snowshoes at the head of the Crean Glacier, winds knocked over several team members and a sled went flying. Luckily, the sled was recovered, but this was just the start of a day where the infamous katabatic winds from the South Pole played havoc with the team. Many times that same day I saw large men, heavily laden with packs, blown over with ease.

The cold was tolerable but the winds were persistent throughout the day. As we crossed the glacier, the gusts were 60-70kmph and several times teams were blown over. Being roped, there was no real danger of losing anyone, but it certainly slowed progress and it took us over three hours to travel only 3km across the glacier.

We had covered 12-13km the previous day, travelling from King Haakon Bay to below the Trident Ridge. We hoped to cover a similar distance today to bring us to Fortuna Bay, but with our slow progress, chances were slim.

In the afternoon, the skies cleared again and we were awestruck by the bright whiteness of the glacier. The scenery was truly awesome and as Fortuna Bay came into view on the horizon, it buoyed our hopes. It finally felt like we were getting there. We still had six miles to go, according to the GPS, but with our objective in sight, spirits were lifted.

The terrain changed a little and the snow had frozen over, with crusts of ice breaking underfoot with every step. It was hard work and people were beginning to tire. We'd been on the move for seven demanding hours, and we probably had another three or four to go. I was anxious to reach Fortuna Bay, where we would be within access of the ship in case of a rescue.

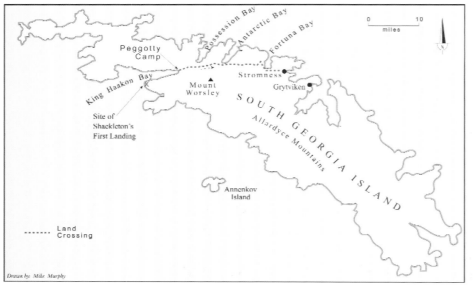

Map of South Georgia showing the route across the island, originally traversed by Shackleton, Worsley and Tom Crean.

Trudging along, we followed the snout of a glacier and crested between Breakwind Ridge and Best Peak. There below us we could see the *Ushuaia*, and what a view! The ship's horn blew in welcome and everyone smiled in relief. No doubt many of us were reflecting on what Crean, Shackleton and Worsley must have gone through, having made this same traverse with none of our special polar clothing, maps or technical gear. That brave team had relied on makeshift crampons fashioned out of nails from their boat, and went without food and sleep. Many of the team were moved to tears thinking of these heroes, and how they must have felt when they heard the 7am bell waking the whaling crews.

It was almost dark by the time we were all safely down on the beach. Support crew from the ship brought three tents to replace the six we lost and we quickly set up camp. The smell of the seals and penguins on the beach would have been intolerable if we were not all so exhausted!

THE TRAVERSE OF SOUTH GEORGIA – DAY 3
On the morning of 15 November we broke camp by 7am. We were thrilled to be joining the entire support team again; the plan was to walk to Stromness to meet them for the final 4 kilometres.

As we headed across Shackleton Valley and above Crean Lake the views were simply amazing. The weather had again turned poor and we walked in cold, misty conditions. But the weather didn't dampen spirits, and as we glissaded down snow slopes the team was buzzing with excitement and pride. Thoughts of Shackleton, Crean and Worsley's grand entrance so many years ago filled our minds. For many of us, it was an emotional experience to be so close to the history we had read and dreamt about. Our first views of the whaling station were of a bleak and lonely spot. The place is uninhabited and the rare tourists are forbidden from wandering around. We went to the graveyard and grouped for a photograph before jumping aboard the Zodiacs and returning to the warmth and safety of the *Ushuaia*. A warm shower, clean clothes and good food were a welcome prize.

It's impossible to convey the atmosphere on board the ship that evening. We started into a sing-song around 9pm, and this lasted into the early hours. Everyone joined in – it was a night we will never forget. While we celebrated, our captain cruised through the dark waters, bringing us to Grytviken.

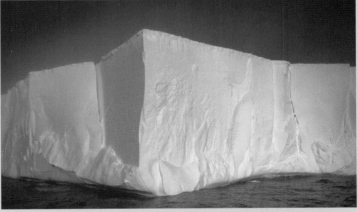

Top: The Murphy children, with Freddy, the expedition mascot, were the youngest members of the expedition. From left, Jack (10), Tim (9), Eve (8).

Middle: A massive tabular iceberg.

Bottom: Elaine Wynn at a king penguin colony in Gold Harbour, South Georgia.

THE CRUISE

Over the next twelve days we continued our amazing journey by ship. Cruising along the Palmer Archipelago, several thousand gentoo penguins waited for us under the dramatic cliffs of Cuverville Island. Sheathbills, Antarctic terns, skuas and blue-eyed shags gazed out from their nests as we cruised slowly by, seemingly as curious about us as we were of them. Before long we were navigating the beautiful Neumayer Channel, enjoying extraordinary vistas of surrounding islands. We landed on Port Lockroy, where bleached whalebones still testify to the harbour's time as a favourite whaling anchorage.

SOUTH SHETLAND ISLANDS AND ANTARCTIC PENINSULA

Rounding off our expedition, we reached the rugged South Shetland Islands. Here, places such as King George Island and Livingston Island support huge numbers of nesting penguins, with seabird rookeries in the cliffs. Elephant seals wallowed all along the shores, threatening us with their pink, fleshy mouths wide open. Nearby Deception Island is still an active volcano, and sailing through the narrow passage into its huge, flooded caldera was a thrilling experience.

Mists were heavy as we approached Elephant Island, where Shackleton's men found refuge during the epic *Endurance* expedition. Watching this ice-covered island come into view was the perfect ending to our expedition.

Dawn at Grytviken, an old whaling station on South Georgia.

Cruising through the icebergs.

The Beyond Endurance team leaving Cape Valentine where Ernest Shackleton first landed to rescue his crew.

Facing page: Point Wilde, Elephant Island, a desolate spit of land where
22 of Shackleton's men spent 4 ½ months awaiting rescue.

A GHOST IN THE MIST

In anticipation we awaited our final challenge. Cruising slowly through the mist, a form began to materialise, like a ghost rising from the icy waters of the Scotia Sea. We were, at last, approaching Elephant Island, where Shacketon's men found refuge during their epic adventure. It took nearly four months and four attempts for Shackleton to rescue the men who remained stranded here. Amazingly, the entire crew of the *Endurance* were found alive.

The highlight of our expedition was the moment we reached Cape Valentine, where Shackleton first landed to rescue his crew. We paid homage to our heroes by landing on the very spit of shore where the crew awaited their boss so many years ago. For me, it was a dream come true to stand in a place that had been etched in my memory from photos I'd seen and books I had read. I was so proud of our team for coming to the Antarctic to pay homage to Irishmen who had achieved an incredible feat of survival. We had succeeded in the first phase of our expedition, and our dream had become a reality.

As I left Elephant Island, my journey was just beginning. Next, I would set out to achieve Shackleton's dream of reaching the South Pole and beyond.

But that will be another story.

There is so much more to say than fits into this book.

These stories are snippets of what happened on expedition. I have been privileged to work with many amazing people. As an adventurer it would be impossible to mention everyone who has helped and encouraged me over the last twenty years.

Many people I have climbed and travelled with had unprecedented, breakthrough points in their careers, some even while on the expeditions described in this book. I could also write an entire book about how I and others would not be alive today but for the heroism and self-sacrifice of people around them. The text in this book is intended only to complement the photographs.

I'd like to thank all team members who have been involved with me in over 60 expeditions and adventures. All contributed to what, for me, were often life-changing and amazing times.

Thanks to my family for their support, trust and belief in my ability to return safely. I know I have given all some scary moments, and without each of you behind me it would have been very different. To Mum and Dad, thank you for giving me the strength to follow my dreams from early in life. I have followed them with conviction and belief.

I'd like to pay special thanks to my close friends Gerry Walsh and Joe O'Leary, for their continuous support and loyal friendship. The honesty and encouragement I receive from both of you is greatly appreciated. Thanks also to my mountaineering mentors and friends Con Moriarty and Val Deane.

Thanks to all my sponsors over the past twenty years of expeditions, climbing and exploring.

To Sidney Pogatchnik, my editor, thanks for her many hours of hard work trying to condense and shape this book with me. Also, thanks to Mark Kroh, our US editor, for his insight and direction.

To the staff at The Collins Press, thanks for their encouragement and belief in my books, and in the climbing and adventuring community as a whole.

Special thanks goes to my staff: Geraldine O'Connor, for keeping my life on track – without your efficiency and patience I would be buried under a mound of paperwork and never achieve my goals; to Niall Foley, thanks for your constant support and competence – I feel lucky to have found someone to work with who contributes so much to my success, whether in the office or on expedition.

PAT FALVEY

IRISH EVEREST SUMMITEERS

#	Summiteer	Route	Country	Summit Date	Time
1	Dawson Stelfox	North Col/Northeast Ridge	Tibet	27 May 1993	10.07
2	Pat Falvey	North Col/Northeast Ridge	Tibet	27 May 1995	09.00
3	Mick Murphy	South Col/Southeast Ridge	Nepal	22 May 2003	09.50
4	Gerard McDonnell	South Col/Southeast Ridge	Nepal	22 May 2003	11.10
5	Terence Bannon	North Col/Northeast Ridge	Tibet	31 May 2003	07.30
6	Clare O'Leary	South Col/Southeast Ridge	Nepal	18 May 2004	6.45
**7	Pat Falvey	South Col/Southeast Ridge	Nepal	18 May 2004	6.45
8	Samantha Carroll	South Col/Southeast Ridge	Nepal	27 May 2004	10.20
9	Humphrey Murphy	North col/Northeast Ridge	Tibet	30 May 2005	07.10
10	Grainne Willis	North Col/Northeast Ridge	Tibet	5 June 2005	06.00
11	Noel Hanna	North Col/Northeast Ridge	Tibet	19 May 2006	09.45
12	Ian McKeever	North Col/Northeast Ridge	Tibet	16 May 2007	12.50
13	Hannah Sheilds	North Col/Northeast Ridge	Tibet	19 May 2007	07.20
14	Bill Hanlon	South Col/Southeast Ridge	Nepal	22 May 2007	08.05
15	Roger McMorrow	South Col/Southeast Ridge	Nepal	23 May 2007	06.30
16	Nigel Hart	South Col/Southeast Ridge	Nepal	23 May 2007	06.30
17	Michael J. O'Dwyer	South Col/Southeast Ridge	Nepal	24 May 2007	07.55

** summited from both Tibet and Nepal

IRISH SUMMITEERS, AMA DABLAM

1	Brendan Murphy	4 April 1990	18.00
2	Mick Murphy	4 April 1991	15.30
3	Pat Falvey	3 Nov 1999	10.30
4	Mick Long	22 Oct 2002	12.00
5	Clare O'Leary	17 May 2006	11.00

IRISH SUMMITEERS, CHO OYU

1-2	Pat Falvey	20 May 1998	12.30
1-2	Gavin Bate	20 May 1998	12.30
3-4	Humphrey Murphy	14 May 2002	14.00
3-4	Richard Dougan	14 May 2002	14.00
5	Grania Willis	27 Oct 2004	08.00
6	Michael O'Dwyer	24 Sept 2005	10.50
7-8	Roger McMorrow	25 Sept 2005	10.10
7-8	Nigel Hart	25 Sept 2005	10.10
9	Patrick Doyle	2 Oct 2006	07.00

Note: The Irish '98 expedition to Cho Oyu was the first Irish team to achieve an oxygen-less ascent of an 8,000-metre peak in an area know to climbers as Death Zone. Story page 107.

Irish climber Adam Cinnamond died on Cho Oyu on return to Base Camp from High Camp between 14 to 16 May 2002. May he rest in peace.

Information compiled by Pat Falvey, to update please contact **www.patfalvey.com**

IRISH SEVEN SUMMIT CLIMBERS

More than 200 mountaineers have climbed all 'Seven Summits' – the highest peak on each of the seven continents.
The first was Dick Bass, an American businessman, who completed the challenge on 30 April, 1985.

Continent	Mountain	Country and/or location	Feet	Height Metres
Asia	Mount Everest	Tibet-Nepal	29,035	8,850
South America	Mount Aconcagua	Argentina	22,834	6,960
North America	Mount McKinley (Denali)	United States, Alaska	20,320	6,194
Africa	Mount Kilimanjaro	Tanzania	19,340	5,995
Europe	Elbrus	Russia/Georgia	18,510	5,642
Antarctica	Vinson Massif	Ellsworth Mts.	16,066	4,897
Australia[1]	Kosciusko	Australia	7,310	2,228

Some climbers believe that the true Seven Summits should include Carstensz Pyramid (16,023 ft.) in Irian Jaya, Indonesia, rather than Australia's Kosciusko.
Carstensz is the highest summit in Australia/Oceania also known as Australasia, but strictly speaking, Australia/Oceania is not a continent.

Irish people to have climbed the Seven Summits

No.	Name	Final Continent	Date	World Ranking	General Comments
1	Pat Falvey	Australia	14 Feb 1997	32nd	
2	Clare O'Leary	Antarctica	16 Dec 2005	119th	First Irish female to complete and 16th worldwide
3	Pat Falvey 2nd	Antarctica	16 Dec 2005	2nd time	Record for completing 7 summits twice including Everest via Tibet and Nepal
4	Ian McKeever	Australia	21 July 2007	208th	World speed record: completing the challenge in the shortest period of time

There are a number of other Irish people trying to complete the Seven Summits at present.
Note: It is estimated that approximately fifteen to 25 people a year are now completing the Seven Summits Challenge.

TEXT INDEX

PHOTO INDEX *(references are to page where caption appears)*